In the Woods with
Adirondack Sportsmen

Hunting the Moose River Drainage

Deer Tracking with the Experts

On the Trapline at Stillwater Reservoir,
Long Lake, Stony Creek & Lows Lake

Robert J. Elinskas

©2014 Robert J. Elinskas
All rights reserved. No part of this book may be reproduced or transmitted in any form by any means without the permission in writing from the publisher.

Printed in the United States of America

ISBN: 978-0-9771017-5-7

Graphics by Cynthia Long

Previous books published by the author include: *A Deer Hunters History Book, Adirondack Camps and Hunts, A Taste of Wild Alaska, Hunting Central NY Whitetail* and *Adirondack Hunters & Trappers.*

Acknowledgements

Into The Woods with Adirondack Sportsmen is my 6th book and is written on wild Adirondack adventures. I had the great privilege of visiting with and gathering the stories from some of the very best sportsmen in the country. In that respect this will be their book much more than mine. It is my wish that this writing will take the reader back into the Adirondacks to rekindle their own memories of the hunt and trapline while enjoying these!

Major contributions were given by Newell Wagoner, Mart and Nancy Allen, Thad Column, Joe DiNitto, Dennis Gipe, Terry and Diane Perkins, Bob Kratzenberg, Raymond Massett, Jim Massett, Tom Massett, Don Hart, Larry Combs, Jim Harter, Johnny Thorpe, Alan Morgan, Rodney Morgan, John Secor, Ben Secor, Kirk McLaughlin, John Pinkos, Tim Dunn, Terry Bostain, and Ken and Mary Hart.

Further support was given by Kerry Rogers, Steve Grabowski, Ladd Hale, Ron Robert, Lynn Roderick, Doris Lamphear and Don Adams.

A special thank you for always being there for help in many forms, my wife Amy, my daughter-in-law, Cassandra, and my graphic artist, Cynthia Long.

Table of Contents

Acknowledgments ...iii
Looking Back – Newell Wagoner ...1
Hunting on the Adirondack League Club
  Thad Column & Mart Allen ...21
The Raymond L. Massett Legacy ...31
  Don Hart ...33
  Ray Hart ...39
  Raymond Massett Jr. ...43
  Jim Massett ...49
  Tom Massett ...59
  Ken Hart ...81
Dennis Gipe ...91
Joe DiNitto ...101
Bob Kratzenberg ...111
Terry Perkins ...127
Trappers Larry Combs & Jim Harter ...145
Johnny Thorpe ...157
Mule Train ...167

Looking Back

Newell Wagoner was born in Boonville, NY, almost 94 years ago on November 8, 1920. A dollar was actually worth a dollar in those days, but they were much harder to earn. Most families had a vegetable garden in their back yard. They also canned a good deal of the produce to use during the winter months. It was much more of a hunter-gatherer generation than it is today. Small game and big game hunting was more "food for the table" than it was a sport. However, for the hunter-gatherer, it was always a joy and a challenge to bag some meat for the table. Most of today's hunters hunt more for the challenge than the meat, as if to test their skill level in the old ways of providing food for your family.

Newell is looking back over 80 years of hunting northern NY. He saw all the changes through the years. His life's work was in Boonville as the co-owner of Wagoner & Hickok Insurance Agency. He was an active member of his community which included being president of the Boonville Oneida County Fair from 1964 through 2004. Newell and Evelyn, his wife of 68 years, still live in his original family home on Schuyler Street. At 93 years, he still drives, mows his own lawn, and maintains a small flower garden. He confessed that he really doesn't know why he got to live so long, because longevity isn't on either side of his family. Newell shared his sporting memories with me that brought him a great deal of pleasure during his years in the field.

In the Beginning

Newell had a very quiet childhood up until he was 10 years old. During his first few grades in school, he was afflicted with some type of physical ailment that was never clearly explained to him. He wasn't allowed to participate in gym classes. He couldn't do anything strenuous, not even ride a bike. His father, John H. Wagoner, would often take him along on work trips just to be sure he stayed quiet.

John was an avid hunter and loved the outdoors. He hunted the Adirondacks every fall for deer and bear. Some of his earliest hunts were up along the Sacandaga River. Even at a young age, Newell loved to hear his stories from deer camp. John gave Newell his first rifle, a .22 caliber autoloader, at age 10. He taught him responsibility, gun safety, and proper gun handling, before and during his first few outings.

Dragging deer out along the Sacandaga River. L to R: Guide Duane Brother, John Miller, John Wagoner, & Mr. McNessor.

John Wagoner was an engineer for Eastern Rock Products. He was very good friends with Harold Owens, who was the company CEO at the time. Blacktop was primarily manufactured at Oriskany Falls, but they had several other satellite quarries. John was involved with building some of those satellite plants and also dealt with supplying various stone aggregates for road construction and improvements. They also experimented with different types of tennis court surfaces. John got to travel around central and northern NY extensively on work projects. Many of his hunting contacts were made at work.

First Buck

Newell took his first buck at a camp owned by Fred Wengil (a former Oneida County Clerk). It was a 2000 acre piece of leased property off the North Lake Road. John, Earl Potts, and Newell hiked in over the old access road early in the season. The road was blocked in several locations with recent windfalls. John and Earl would cut them out with a crosscut saw as they came to them. It took them 3 hours to reach the tar-papered cabin. The cabin would accommodate six hunters. Once the stove was running and the lamps were lit, Newell could see that the cabin

John H. Wagoner (Newell's father) on left and Earl Potts with Newell's first buck on 28 Oct 1934, a 10-pointer! (Family photo)

was well set-up and comfortable. Supplies and deer were hauled to and from the cabin by a local farmer with a team and wagon.

In the morning, they walked the trails. There were 2 main circular trails with painted blazes, one red and one blue. Then John and Earl put on a short drive for Newell. His father told him, "Don't shoot anything unless you can see antlers above its ears!" When the drive got underway, this deer came out and Newell didn't have any problem seeing antlers. He shot and the buck went down shortly afterwards. His first buck was a 10-pointer! The men dragged it out to the cabin that day, October 28, 1934.

Hunting Out of Avery's Hotel

Lyman Avery was road supervisor in the town of Arietta. He would purchase crushed stone and other road improvement products from the Newport Quarry.

This is where John first met Lyman. John and Clyde Powers (a fellow employee) went up to Avery's Hotel on Route 10 in 1936. They enjoyed their hunt and returned for the next 3 seasons. John brought Newell along with him during 1937 and 1938, when he was in his last 2 years of high school. Newell gave me his impression of hunting at Avery's.

The hunt at Avery's was very different than a traditional hunt. There were 45 or 50 men participating in each hunt. He remembers the bartender, "Stubby," and also Bobby Avery, since he was about his own age.

Something he never forgot was the memory of 4 middle-aged men that always sat together at their own table. They hunted as a group, each one with a mauser rifle, and would often converse in German. Sometimes they would be dressed in a military uniform. Newell asked his father about them and John replied that they were members of The American Nazi Party. This was well before WWII and Newell often wondered what became of them during and after the war.

Breakfast was being served by 5 AM. Some days they would have to cross the west branch of the Sacandaga River in a row boat with 4 or 5 other men. Newell was impressed to see that if a deer was wounded, they would work very hard to try finding it and finish it off. Newell hit a buck on one drive and Bob Avery and another person tracked it right 'til dark, but didn't get it. The younger hunters did most of the pushing on drives, usually about 16 or 17 pushers and the rest as watchers. There was a lot of deer in the woods in those days, so a lot of deer were moved. Newell couldn't see how any bucks would get away, but they sure did. The stories being told afterwards were always fun to hear. He kept a brief diary of his first trip out to Avery's. Here is Avery's Hotel in 1937, through the eyes of a 17 year-old hunter.

Diary at Avery's

Wednesday, November 10, 1937

Got up early and did school work. Went to school, studied, and worked very hard in every class. I guess we are leaving tonight for Avery's. I hope so. After school, I did some school work and soon ate supper. After supper, I went down street. Got shells for gun, gloves, socks, etc. Came home and packed. Dottie Brown arrived to stay a while. Went over to dance and hung around. Came home and found Bus Brown here. Had a bit to eat. Packed car and said good-bye. Left at 12 or later. Arrived at Avery's at 2:00 AM. People still up. Nice place as far as I can see. Retired very early in the morning-cool.

Thursday, November 11, 1937

Got up early and ate. Got a nice place here. Looked everything over. Very cold. Went up in back of Hotel for hunt. On first drive, I had watch point at edge of lake. Nice watch point. I stayed on that watch point for 3 long, cold hours! Then we made a drive further over and in whole day not much gotten. A long, long, walk back out. Walked for 2 ½ hours steady to get back to Hotel and boy, oh boy that was some walk. Moonlight helped a lot. Spent a nice time eating. Excellent food. Clyde came in early and now we have four in our crowd. Meeting a good many people up here. Retired-cold.

Friday, November 12, 1937

Up early and ate breakfast. Bus is terribly sick and I don't mean maybe. Went to Shaker Place. Bus didn't. Crossed river and made long walk to Moose Mtn. Lyman, Bobby, Brad, Ray, Mil, and I drive from top of Mtn. Ray shot a ----? Brad on my other side thought I shot and had found a buck. I walked up to him and deer was still alive. He was wounded. We followed him for a long time, but lost his tracks at the creek. Came back and then Bobby, Lyman and I went across Moose Creek and were on watches. The others were below. The drive came through and us watchers joined the drive. Lisse Thisse got a 6-point, Dad shot an 8-point, Bill Thisse got a 10-point. One shot on drive also got some meat. Left deer half way out. Got up to Shaker Place way after dark. Moonlight helped. Got acquainted that evening with the boys. Retired late-raining out.

Saturday, November 13, 1937

Got up and it is still raining. Ate breakfast. Everybody doubtful about going out. Finally we started. Down to Ash Mtn. I was on watch. Drive came through. Plenty of shooting. Milton Avery shot a buck while driving. Then we found out another gang was driving into us and one of their watchers shot a spike horn from our drive. Then we made another crazy drive and quit. Started back to Shaker Place. Rained all the time. I was soaked. Back at Hotel, we changed clothes and started drying them. Ate supper and a fine one it was. Spent evening talking. At midnight had a grand party. Clams, etc in the kitchen. Then all the men washed and wiped the dishes. Rain.

Sunday, November 14, 1937

Up early and had breakfast. Headed for Shaker Place. Crossed river and headed for Ash Ridge where 4 deer were shot Friday. I watched and at noon the drive ended. Nothing shot. Then we started and drove to Three Sisters Mtn, Teaville Swamp, and Round Top Mtn. No deer. Back and crossed Moose River. Went after deer – Dad's, Bill Tissie's, and meat. Brought them down to Shaker Place. They brought deer up river by boat. Hid the deer by river and brought Dad's deer up to Hotel after dark. Called Mother and told her we were going to hunt tomorrow. She didn't like that. Ate supper and spent evening talking. Retired very late and bed felt good. Fair and cool.

Monday, November 15, 1937

Got up at 6 AM and dressed. Went down to breakfast. Grabbed sandwiches and started for Shaker Place. A large crowd. 39 or so hunters. Crossed river in terrible boat. Went up to Cow Creek Valley. Watchers put out around Moose Mtn. Drivers came through and Bus (above me) did not shoot at buck and bear that passed him. One fellow shot at the bear and wounded it. Johnson of RI shot a nice 8-point. Heavy buck. Then watchers headed for Buck Mtn. Stubby and I are last watchers. I could hear deer, but could not see them. Hoped for drivers to drive them out, but no drivers came. They couldn't see on top of Mtn because of snow and fog. Stubby missed a crotch horn. Went back to river, crossed and back to hotel. Bobby Avery got a nice buck, but didn't get in until very late. Ate supper and sat around. Packed up and put deer on car. On way home saw a big buck in road with 2 doe. Home by 1 AM.

<end of journal>

In the fall of 1939, Newell was enrolled at Amherst College in Massachusetts and was unable to make the hunt at Avery's. He did receive a card from his father and fellow hunters on his birthday, November 8, 1939. It was signed by Clyde, Lyman Avery, and 8 others in the group that he knew. It briefly got him a little "homesick" for the annual hunt.

In the early days, they also hunted the "Hogs Back" off Hawkinsville Road almost to Woodgate. These hunters were mostly local people around Boonville. They put on drives to get the deer moving and young Newell was shocked to see that does were occasionally taken. John reminded him that "what happens in the woods, stays in the woods." The reasoning was, people had families, times were tough, and there were a lot of deer. No one wanted to get caught either, so they were very careful on getting the meat back to town. The illegal deer were hung in a garage by a small house within sight of Woodgate Corners. The deer was cut into large sections or quarters and put into a feed bag with a shoulder sling. One of their party had a rumble seat on the back of a Model T Ford. After dark, on the way back to town, one guy would ride back there with the venison and if they saw a car in the distance coming, the venison would be slung off into the bar ditch. After the car passed and all was clear, they would loop around and get the meat. The illegal venison would always get John's wife upset and nervous.

1932-1944

John used to drive into Utica almost every day and he had a routine that he followed on the way down and back. People knew he would be going down and back, so he would regularly give people a ride into Utica to do their business and then bring them back when his work was done. Before leaving, he would stop at the Boonville drugstore for cigarettes. Anyone heading for Utica would meet him there. Then it was across the street to Crook & Brook's Service station for fuel. It was an hour trip over the old road (Route 12) to Utica.

Trume Haskell had a service and repair station in Barneveld village, so if he had any repairs needed, he would often go there. John was no stranger at Trume's camp on West Canada Creek. He hunted out of his camp for a couple of seasons with Newell and several of his friends. They hunted hard days, but evenings it was drinking, smoking, playing cards, and telling stories. Newell remembers one fellow that always seemed to overdo it on drinking and the guys would often play jokes on him. One evening, they tied his shoes together to trip him up and another time they exchanged his ammo for some that wouldn't fit in his rifle.

John would often do the cooking in camp. One evening when the meal was just getting started, Newell was sent out to the "cache" for 2 cans of tomato soup. The "cache" was out and away from the buildings and kind of dug into a hillside. It was a safe place to store food and keep it from freezing. When he got out to the cache and opened the door, he was shocked to see several doe laid out behind the canned goods. On telling John about it, he was reminded again, "what you see at camp, stays at camp!"

On the following weekend, there was about 18 guys in camp and ready to sit down to a venison supper. Then came 3 or 4 loud knocks at the door and in comes 2 state game wardens. Newell got a little nervous, but they came in and sat down to supper and visited with everyone. He didn't think the wardens knew of the cache or what was in it either. Newell really enjoyed himself at Haskell's, especially watching how the older generation operated.

Newell had always hunted with his father. Hunting plans and trips were always formulated before the fall hunting seasons opened. In February of 1944, John was tragically killed in a traffic accident on Route 12, Deerfield Hill. The death of his father left Newell devastated. He had been very close to his father and the past 10 years of hunting together created many fine memories. As fall approached, he made no plans for hunting and was undecided whether to go or not.

When deer season opened up, Earl Potts called Newell and asked him if he wanted to go deer hunting with him. Potts, from Prospect, was a mechanic for Eastern Rock Products, had worked with John and also hunted with him. Newell agreed to go and that weekend they hunted some of the ridges and hills that bordered the Bear Creek Road out of Woodgate. Once in the woods, Newell realized how good it was to get back out on the hunt again and forget about everything else. They enjoyed some pretty good luck in there, which revived his spirit for the hunt. The following years saw Newell hunting with some of his own personal friends. One of his closest friends was Frank Buscall.

John H. Wagoner Newell's father. (Family photo)

Frank Buscall

Newell hunted with Frank Buscall for over 40 years. Frank was older and was Newell's high school physical education teacher. Before that, Frank had played baseball for the Rome Colonels in the Canadian-American League. The 2 men developed a style of hunting that put an amazing amount of bucks on the game pole. They would have a destination in mind on starting out for the hunt. Then one of them would begin hunting in that direction. After 15 minutes, he would find a good place to watch while the second man would begin hunting along on his tracks. Once the second hunter caught up to the first, he would continue on for 15 minutes more and wait for the first hunter to catch up. They killed many fine bucks looping around behind the first hunter to get the scent of what just walked quietly by in the distance, bucks the first hunter was never aware of, but ran right into the second man.

Buck Down

On one hunt, Newell and Frank met and planned their next line of the hunt. Newell had just started away when Frank gave a low whistle and pointed. A minute or so passed and then he shot. He hollered to Newell, "He's down." They walked over and it was a spike horn. Frank was in a hurry to get out of the woods because it was Election Day and he lived in Lansingburgh, north of Troy. They put their rifles against a tree and were about to dress out the buck when it suddenly jumped up, gave a quick look at the two hunters, and sped off into the cover. They tracked the buck a short distance, but he was pretty healthy. Frank made it home to vote on time. Newell's brother showed up at his home just before dark with a buck on his car. Bob Wagoner lived in Clinton and had been hunting in the same general area that Frank and Newell were that day. His buck was a familiar looking spike horn that had a very recent bullet scar, ½ inch deep across its forehead. Brother Bob was a Pharmacist and managed to buy his own drug store there. He developed some serious heart problems and past on early, at 42 years of age.

Hunting Limekiln Lake Area (1955-1960)

In 1955, Newell and several business men from the Boonville area leased some land from the Adirondack League Club. The club had plans to log the property and then sell it to get it off their tax rolls. The lease included a few cabins. Accessing the cabins involved a boat ride down the length of Limekiln Lake from the parking area and then a 15 minute walk down the outlet. Most of the trips into the camp were pleasant and uneventful, but there was one trip down the lake that he will never forget.

It was Veteran's Day weekend. At first light in the morning, a brisk wind was blowing down the lake when they left shore. There were 3 men in the boat dressed in woolies and long-johns, and pack baskets on the floor. The waves hitting the bow sent up a drenching spray that couldn't be avoided no matter how they ran the boat. At the far end, they were all sopping wet and cold for the pack down to camp. They got the woodstove going and the kitchen stove, too. They all stripped down and wrung out their clothing. It took what seemed like forever to dry the clothes. They started with their underwear, then pants, and then shirts. The Woolrich parkas took the longest, especially when you wanted to be out in the woods hunting. It took until 10 o'clock that night to get everything dry! Meanwhile, the weather was turning sharply colder.

The next morning, they were all out hunting at first light. A hunt was made on the ridge above the lake. Newell remembers looking down at the lake through the trees and noticing that the water color had changed. He was thinking, "what's the matter with that lake? The water doesn't look natural." Well, when he got closer, he realized that it was frozen. They had Monday off because of the holiday, but they had taken 2 bucks. They had to drag them up to the lake and then along the shore all the way to the car.

One weekend, they tried to drive deer down a mountainside that had just been logged. There were tree tops laying every which way and bent over slashings to further clutter up the landscape. Harold Sweeney and Al Toth were added to the group on this weekend. Al was a good woodsman and an excellent deer hunter. Al and Harold were pushing deer with Newell, Frank Buscall, and Bobby Toth on watch. During the drive 2 bucks came running through the fallen tops near Newell. He fired twice, missing both times. Then 5 more shots were heard from the other watchers. When they regrouped, it was learned that everyone had missed. Al stated, "If you guys can't shoot straight, I'm not hunting with you anymore!"

1955
Frank Buscall
Limekiln Lake

Cabin below Limekiln Lake outlet.

Logging Camp across from Limekiln Lake on former ADK League property. Al Toth was logging camp boss.

George Olney with buck taken on drive at Limekiln Lake.

The next morning, Newell was back up on the same ridge line. A shot rang out in the woods above him. Shortly afterwards, he could see a buck walking in his direction. It appeared to be hurt and had a huge bulge on the side of its body. Newell let it walk to within 100 feet and then dropped it with one shot with his .35 Remington. He was looking over the 8-pointer when this fellow, Charlie Murray, came huffing and puffing along on the buck's tracks. The fellow said, "I'm glad you put him down. I wounded him up above here, so he's my buck!" Newell replied, "I don't think so. He was healthy enough to walk down here on all 4 legs, so he's my buck!" About that time, Al Toth came along. Al was also in charge of the current logging operations there. They asked Al, "Who gets the deer?" Al said, "The rules I operate with is, whoever stops the deer, gets the deer!" They took one more buck that day. Al's faith in their shooting ability being restored. They dragged Newell's buck only a short distance to a logging road and Al told them to leave it right there. He had a load of logs heading up toward Boonville the next day. The truck showed up as promised, backed into Newell's driveway, and dropped off the buck. It doesn't get any easier than that!

Newell was good friends with the Sweeney brothers from Lyons Falls. They were loggers and had a good-sized operation. He hunted with them at their logging

Blackjack Camp on Abby Road, L to R: Bill Hitzelburger & Joe Pieffer, owned by Harold & Vern Sweeney.

camp near Inlet in Hamilton County and later, in Lewis County, Lyonsdale Township. The Sweeney's purchased 2500 acres in that area and removed some of the hunting clubs. Newell and his friends set up the Black Jack hunting camp in a small cabin on the property. When Sweeney purchased the property, it had been only selectively logged, but then he went and intensely logged it. This created a thick tangle of cover that the deer would run to when stressed. Brantingham Lake lay just to the north with fairly open timber all the way. When the season opened, hunters from camps around Brantingham would enter the woods and start deer. Most of these deer would head straight for the thick cover on Sweeney's property. Newell and his friends would be on all the active runs entering the heavily logged property. Newell said one morning he counted 19 doe go by before he finally shot a buck.

While hunting out of Blackjack Lodge a heavy snowfall began. Their hunting group gathered and decided to return to camp. Visibility was very poor. Newell was leading the group when he saw a big buck rise from it's bed only 20 feet away and run. He fired a hasty shot with his .35 Remington and the buck dropped. They couldn't find a bullet hole anywhere on the 10-point buck, and claimed he scared him to death! Later it was discovered the bullet had entered through the ear and stayed in the head.

Newell with the Snowstorm Buck.

The Great Windfall

On November 25, 1950, Newell was hunting with an acquaintance named Lincoln White. They were going to hunt an area near North Wilmurt. Newell was driving his 1949 Buick Special when he pulled off the road and parked along Farr Road. It was just starting to get light outside, but there was a strong breeze blowing. He didn't think much of it because the wind often dies down when the sun comes up. The men entered the woods and worked their way up towards a ridge they planned to hunt. On the ridge the wind was building in strength, occasionally pushing over trees or snapping off sizable tree limbs with a loud "POP." They decided to hunt the lower elevations and hopefully escape the stronger wind gusts.

As they went lower, the winds became stronger yet. Large trees were being pushed over with huge root structures standing on end. Both men agreed the woods were too dangerous to be in! They unloaded their rifles and spread out for safety on the way out to the Buick. Newell saw 2 deer on the trip out and he thought they were more concerned about falling trees than anything else. Out at the car, an 18 inch diameter hardwood tree had fallen parallel with it, and real close, but never touched it. When they looked down the road, all they could see were windfalls across it. Now what do we do??

They were discussing what options they had, when a small caravan of vehicles (all people trying to get out) came down the road. These people were all panic stricken by the storm and blocked roads. Newell and Lincoln joined the caravan. Between them, they had 1 axe and 2 crosscut saws. They divided themselves into teams to work on each windfall. They would limb and cut an opening just big enough for a car to pass through and then move onto the next. They did this all the way down to Goldie Robert's place near the Wheelertown Road. Eventually they got to Forestport and the wider state maintained areas.

Newell walked into the family kitchen at about 5:30 PM. When his mother saw him, she said, "Where's your brother?" He replied, "How would I know? I have been gone all day." She replied, "I brought him over this morning and dropped him off by your car. We left a note on your windshield. You've got to go back and get him!" He shot back, "Mother, there is no way I'm going back up that road tonight. He's going to have to figure his own way home!" Bob came home about 10:30 PM that evening. He failed to leave a note on the car and he came out after Newell left. They all agreed it was a very scary day and were very thankful nobody was injured.

The Black River Hunt

It was the last day of deer season and Frank Buscall hadn't tagged a buck yet. Newell suggested they try one of their old haunts, up along the Black River off Farr Road. Arriving, they saw a good foot of snow on the ground. Also, the road hadn't been plowed recently.

They parked the car on the side of the road and headed off into the woods. With a foot of snow, it took considerable effort just to get around. Furthermore, nothing was moving. No fresh tracks or sign of any kind. They could see the lights of the Forestport Tower on the North Lake Road above the distant tree line. About 2:30 PM, they regrouped back at the car for some hot coffee and a sandwich. Newell's hips were beginning to hurt with all the deep snow walking. Both men worked up a pretty good sweat, so they shed their parkas, gloves, and hats to cool off. Things were not looking so good for Frank using his deer tag. They decided to spend the remainder of the day between Farr Road and Black River.

Newell with a head mount given to him by Frank Buscall. Frank was his hunting partner for 40 years. When Buscall's home and furnishing were sold before they moved south, Newell was given the head. (Bob Elinskas photo)

After a good long break, the men entered the woods on the river side of the road. Their target was a small flat above the river where deer sometimes bedded. Newell was leading the way as they entered the flat. He was thinking, "This is crazy! My hips are hurting. I'm tired and the day is almost over. We should be heading home!" Suddenly Frank shot right behind him. Newell said, "It scared me so bad! I never jumped so high in my life!" He turned around and saw a flash of brown and Frank fired again. He shouted to Newell, "A real nice buck!" They went over and found where one bullet had passed through a 4 inch tree, but there was blood in the tracks with 2 shots fired. They decided to wait for a while and let both them and the deer calm down.

After a half hour, Frank said, "I'll take his track and you go over to the river in case it tries to cross. The buck had bedded on a little ridge over looking the flat the men were on. He had been watching them while they waited, but he was hurt bad. Newell got over to the river, but it was about 150 feet down a steep bank to get there. Frank jumped the buck and fired twice more. Then Newell could see the buck struggling to cross the river. He didn't want to finish him in the water. When the buck climbed out on the far bank, it sat down on it's ass, much like a dog would, and Newell could see that the buck didn't have any battery left. "Frank was right, " he thought, "That buck has a fine set of antlers."

Frank followed the buck right down to the water and then hooked up with Newell. The buck was all but dead across the river and there was no easy way over, but straight across. In they went, walking on slippery rocks. The water was icy cold, but not over knee deep. They grabbed the buck and immediately brought him back across. Then they dressed him and left him. Now it was full dark. They walked out to the car and left rifles and parkas. Then it was back into the woods with flashlights for the buck. The steep slope up from the river and the deep snow brought out a heavy sweat on the men. They had it loaded on the car by 7:30 PM. Frank finally tagged out and Newell was damn glad deer season was over!

Fishing Trips

Newell's sporting adventures were not limited to fall deer hunting. Many day trips were made out to the area streams, ponds, and lakes. He became a skillful fisherman with bait, spinners and flies. Karl Kornmeyer was a good friend of his. Newell claimed that Karl made him 6 of the most effective trout flies that he ever used. They were all lost in the course of trout fishing. The last one wasn't lost on a trout. He was fishing the upper reaches of Pine Brook in a boggy area, when one of his casts landed the fly behind a clump of grass. When he straightened the line, and gave a tug, a muskrat swam out from the grass with the fly firmly attached to its back. It was good-bye fly!

Newell told me of a late May fishing trip over Decoration Day weekend, on the upper West Canada Creek. It was in 1939 and Eastern Rock Products were experimenting with some cork infused "CorkTurf" tennis court surfaces. Officials at the Rockefeller Center in NY City were interested in trying some out. John Wagoner was involved with negotiations. John was asked if he had any trout fishing up in his neck of the woods. There was lots of interest with the Rockefeller officials, so the trip into Trume Haskell's camp was arranged. John and Newell were along with the group over the weekend. Newell remembered the weather being cool and the water a little high, so conditions were not ideal. Yet everyone caught trout, averaging 7 to 9 inches. Only a few were longer. The trip in general was very enjoyable.

Newell also told me of a springtime trip into Horn Lake. It was a remote Adirondack lake and the trout fishing was rumored to be excellent. Sedric Freeman was to be his fishing companion on the trip. They made arrangements with Bus Bird at Sixth Lake to fly them in for a few days of fishing. Bus kept a small boat and also a canoe on the lake that they could use. On May 19th, they were on the shore of Horn Lake unloading their outfit from the aircraft. Spring came late this year with the ground still frozen rock hard. After a couple of hours work, they had a comfortable camp set up with a good supply of dry firewood.

They soon found out that the trout were hitting. Most of the fish were being

Buster Bird at Horn Lake

Camp at Horn Lake

*Sedric Freeman &
Horn Lake Brookies*

caught along the shoreline windfalls; big, lively, healthy brook trout. The weather was fair and the scenery pristine. Life was good.

Their first full day on the lake was Monday. They had just nicely started fishing when they heard this loud bang. Sedric said, "That sounded like a car door slamming!" Across the lake near the old Adirondack League Club dock, they could see 3 men getting out of a Niagara Mohawk pick-up truck. One walked out on the dock and shouted, "Where's the boat?" Newell told them and shortly afterwards they began fishing the other end of the lake with Bus's boat and one they brought in with them.

While the 3 men were fishing, Newell and Sedric did some investigating. These NiMo employees had driven a 4-wheel drive company vehicle over a posted road all the way from Moose River Plains. Sharing the lake with other fishermen, even in this remote wilderness setting is quite tolerable, but sharing it with someone breaking all the rules and doing it on company time just rubbed them the wrong way. They got the license plate number off the pickup and turned it over to their pilot. On the flight out, they followed their muddy tire tracks all the way out to the plains

Newell Wagoner on Horn Lake

road. They heard afterward that the employees were all called in to account for this, but didn't hear any final outcome. Aside from this, the fishing and camping trip into Horn Lake was a good getaway. They also hiked through woods to stretch their legs. Pockets of snow could still be found in the shaded areas, so they packed their catch in snow for the trip out.

At 93 years of age, Newell's hunting years were over a decade or so past. At times, he wonders what hunting is turning into in some areas. He sees trucks go by with multiple ATVs trailered behind heading for High Market and other parts of Tug Hill. Few hunters seem to be willing to walk or even drag a deer any distance. Everything seems to change in time. Newell is from the old school. He feels very blessed and grateful for the time frame he was able to hunt in and experience during his life.

Hunting on the Adirondack League Club

The Adirondack League Club was created in 1890 by a group of affluent, conservation-minded sportsmen. They wanted a place where they could preserve and enjoy the Adirondack environment to its fullest. For the last 123 years, that is exactly what they have done. Hunting and fishing on club property was always rumored to be the very best. As active Adirondack sportsmen, we often wonder what hunting on the various private holdings within the park was like. In the spring of 2013, I visited with Thad Column at his home in Fayetteville. Thad is a current club member who owns a camp on Little Moose Lake. I also visited with Mart Allen at his home on the middle branch of the Moose River. These interviews may give the reader more insight on how hunting was conducted on the club, at least during the 1960s.

Interior of Thad Column's boathouse above the slips. (Bob Elinskas photo)

View from the boathouse – Little Moose Lake and Panther Mountain. (Bob Elinskas photo)

Thad Column was introduced to the club through his father, Thad L. Column. Thad Sr. would hunt every fall out of Jack Hunter's camp. Jack was a close family friend of the Column's. Thad's son got out of the Navy in 1964. He began a plastering business in the Syracuse area shortly afterward. He bid on large contracts, hospitals, office buildings, etc., and did very well with it. In 1984, he bought a camp overlooking Little Moose Lake with a large boathouse on the shoreline below it. There were 3 comfortable guest cabins also, but the boathouse was the centerpiece of his holdings. He put a new roof on it, added spacious decks, rebuilt the chimney, and added many new upgrades. It was pure Adirondack and his pride and joy. He did most of his entertaining here.

Thad began hunting the club in 1954 with his father at Jack Hunter's place. He remembers the hunts as being very productive right through the 1970s. His father was a more avid hunter than he was, but no one enjoyed camp and the flavor of the Adirondacks more than Thad Jr., he always had a few stories to share about the people that guided them each season.

John's Sister

Late one afternoon, while out on a hunt, Thad wounded a small buck on the Bisby Club. They had snow cover and felt the buck would not go far. Since it was late, they decided to return to camp over at Jack Hunter's. They would have supper and let the deer succumb. After the meal, Pitt Smith and another guide, John, came back to get the deer. There was no problem finding the deer and they soon had it dressed and loaded. On the way back, they decided to take it off the club property, but had to get it through the gate. The club was very strict on transporting deer off the club. Pitt stopped the truck just short of the gatehouse and out of sight. They put the deer between them then draped a Woolrich parka around it nice and natural-like. Finally, they put a woolen hat on the head and tucked the ears inside.

When they pulled up to the gate, Leo Minne walked outside to the truck. He took a quick peek inside and then straightened up. Pitt was the driver and Leo whispered to him, "Who's that in the middle?" Pitt replied, "Oh, that's John's sister." Leo whispered, "My God! That's the ugliest woman that I have ever seen!" The gate went up and the truck pulled away with its three passengers. Two of them were laughing hysterically!

Norm Villiere

Thad had a great admiration for Norm Villiere. Norm was often hired as one of their guides. Lunch was usually taken at some out building or somebody's camp. While chowing down, Norm would be telling one story after another, keeping everyone entertained.

Tough Getting a Full Night's Sleep

Norm had just nicely gotten to sleep one evening when he was awakened by a noise downstairs. He was the only one home, so he listened more. He could hear things falling on the kitchen floor. "Damn, that sounds like a bear!" he thought. He grabbed his rifle, slipped in some shells, and then quietly went downstairs. He surprised the bear which then proceeded to make a speedy retreat out of the window it came in through. Norm shot the bear and it died while hanging half in and half out of the window. Norm was all cleaned up and had just left a warm, comfortable bed. He sure as hell didn't want to get involved with a stinky damn bear in the middle of the night, so he left it right there. He went back upstairs and was soon asleep.

Around 6 AM, his wife Judy came home. When she walked into the kitchen and turned on the light, Norm was awakened this time by a blood-curdling scream. The sight of the bear in the window, with blood stains draining down the wall and the floor was quite a shock for her. Norm began the bear burglary cleanup immediately afterwards!

Thad told me that Norm had no fear of nature's elements, either. Thad shot a buck one November when it was damn cold out. The buck died right in the middle of the Moose River. Norm waded right out without hesitation and pulled it to the shore.

A Real Good Dog

Thad used to enjoy going after grouse in the fall. The trouble was, as much as he enjoyed it, he was a damn poor shot. He rarely brought home a bird. A friend of his, who was an avid duck hunter, suggested he try hunting ducks. He further offered him the use of his labrador retriever. A few locations were recommended and Thad decided to try his luck along Oneida Lake.

When duck season opened, Thad drove over to his buddy's house and picked up his lab, who was very excited to go. He drove out to a familiar bay on the lake and set up a small blind in the cattails. He noticed that there were other hunters in the bay, all set up and ready for the ducks. Whenever a flight of ducks would pass over, everyone would shoot and some ducks would fall to the water. The lab would then charge out into the water and bring him back a duck every time. Thad said, "I couldn't hit a duck to save my ass," but that lab brought me my limit in ducks by mid-morning, so I went home.

Thad still enjoys his camp on Little Moose Lake. It is a peaceful, beautiful area, full of good memories of times past. I told him I planned on talking with Mart Allen about some of his years on the club. Thad told me that Mart was very good for the club and that he would be a good man to visit with. Thad finished by saying that Mart turned the forestry program right around and the club made money every year he ran it.

Mart Allen

Several months later I had my visit with 87 year-old Mart. Central Adirondack people need no introduction, but for those of you who do, I will brief you. Mart knows the Adirondacks well and from many perspectives. He had his head in the woods since he was a school boy running his own trapline. After a hitch in the Army, he enrolled at the NY State Ranger School at Wanakena, NY, in 1950. He graduated a year later and worked at various Central NY locations while trapping the Adirondacks winters. It wasn't until 1958, that he made a more permanent move into the mountains. Mart happened to be one of the first men awarded the position of NY State Forest Ranger in an open competitive civil service exam. Before this, they were all politically appointed. He was assigned to the Old Forge district.

Mart with daughter, Nancy & son, Marty Jr. & a very early snowmobile. (Allen photo)

Mart in front of Warden Camp, south branch of Moose River. April 1960 Trapline Camp. (Allen photo)

This position opened many new doors for him. He got to know a large number of local people. This included many Adirondack League Club members. In time, he was given permission to trap on club property. Also, there were opportunities to pick up a few extra bucks guiding on the club. In the early 1960s, Mart obtained his guide license. His boss wasn't very comfortable seeing his Forest Ranger guiding, but Mart argued, "What I do off the state clock is my own business!"

Just about all of his guiding was done on club property. The League Club members are mostly business and professional people. They enjoy their privacy and most of them are not what you would consider "hard core hunters." Jack Hunter's camp was a frequent destination for Mart during deer season. Jack Hunter and his guests would hire four or five guides to push deer for them. There were a lot of deer on the club, right through the 1970s. Hunter success, even for an unskilled hunter, ran high. Some of the regular guides were Pit Smith, Artie Baker, Norm Villiere, Bob Goodsell, Mart Allen, and Red Perkins. Back in those days, few if any, hunters or guides carried cameras. Any photographs were most likely to be taken back at camp, after the deer were hung.

The first time Mart started guiding with the group, some of the fellows didn't know Mart was a State Forest Ranger. A couple of them began talking about one of their adventures that wouldn't pass the "legal test." Red Perkins told them to

4 - 8-pointers, Jack Hunter's camp on Adirondack League Club. L to R: Thad L. Column, John Albright, Jack Hunter, & Charlie Harden. (Column family photo)

shut up! Mart informed them that he didn't want to be involved in anything illegal and if they were, he didn't want to hear about it. The guides were paid $25.00 a day and were sometimes given a big tip.

Dressed and Down, in That Order

Mart remembers one hunt where he was pushing deer with Reg Villiere, Artie Baker, and Red Perkins near the outlet of Little Moose Lake. Mart was nearing the end of the push when this 6-pointer came running back at him. Some of the pushers had already come out to the line of watchers and he could hear them talking in the distance. He slapped a couple of trees real hard with a stick he carried and turned the buck back. Then Mart threw the stick at him and shouted, "Here comes a buck! It's OK to shoot, I'm behind a tree."

Thad Column, Sr. saw the buck turn and run straight away, heading for the outlet. He fired once at the fleeing buck. Mart could see the buck when the shot rang out and he saw it stumble briefly. Mart and Artie walked over to the deer's track and here is this big steamy pile of guts. The whole paunch! Column and the other hunters walked up to the pile and Mart replied, "You won't have to worry about finding this

Guides with deer taken at Jack Hunter's camp on Adirondack League Club. L to R: Pitt Smith, Red Perkins & Bob Goodsel. (Column family photo)

deer. He's not going far!" Column said, "That's not from the deer I shot at!" To which Mart replied, "The hell it isn't! I saw the buck when you hit it!" The outlet stream was just beyond them. They found the buck lying in the water on the far side.

They used to guide George Raymond. He operated the Raymond Forklift Co. in Greene, NY. George was really into deer hunting in the 60s. He would have just Mart and Artie Baker for guides and eight hunters. Besides their buck tags, they all had party permits. There were a lot of deer taken at this camp.

Guiding for Jack Hunter or Thad Column's group, there would be four or five guides. One thing about hunting on the club, everyone went to a camp and had a hot lunch. All had hot consomme soup or broth to go with the sandwiches. With Raymond's group, they would place all the watchers, and then Mart and Artie would go in and get the deer moving. Mart never believed in barking or making any vocal noises during a drive, but he would crack limbs and brush and whack trees with sticks. He always told the group, "Be sure you are looking at a deer before you go pointing your rifle. If a doe comes out, even if you have a permit, don't be too quick to shoot. Often a buck is right behind her." On one drive, Mart was almost out to the line and still cracking sticks. He looked ahead and a Dr. Kilroy had his rifle sights right on Mart. The doctor brought his rifle right down when he saw Mart clearly. It happened that three or four does had come crashing by the doctor only a minute earlier. When he heard Mart coming, he was thinking, "It must be the buck!" Mart said, "It gives you a very eerie feeling to have a loaded rifle pointed at you!"

Some real trophy heads were among the bucks taken during Mart's guiding years. One of the biggest racks should have been taken by Thad Column, Sr., but was lost. The guides pushed it out to him on a warm and balmy November day. Thad was using a .300 Savage and he was good with it. He didn't miss! Well, he hit this big buck and he must have paunched it. The guides searched all over the area and couldn't come up with it.

About 2 weeks later, Mart was guiding 2 men out of George Oswald's camp in the same general area. Mart wandered right onto that big lost buck. It was a gorgeous 10-point rack, a real Adirondack trophy. He cut the head off the carcass and wound up giving the head to one of the clients.

I Just Couldn't Do It

Mart told me he had a real problem trying to hunt deer on the club property. He fed 100 or more deer every winter right in his front yard. He just couldn't bring himself to kill one of them. One November, he was a mile or so away from his home, cutting brush along one of the roads. Around noon, he drove home for lunch. After lunch, he returned to continue cutting brush. There was a couple inches of snow cover and there at his work site, a buck had walked over and hooked up a 2" sapling. He saw the buck's tracks cross the road and he thought, "The heck with this, I'm going hunting!"

He went back home and got his rifle. He told his wife Nancy, that he was going to get his buck today. She was to drop him off by the track when she went to pick the kids up from school. Well, Mart got on that buck's track, like a coon hound on a hot track. He tracked that buck for a mile or so, all the way back to his own backyard. The buck was bedded down under the kids' swing set! He just walked into the house and put his gun away!

Back in the 60s, they used to take 65 deer a season off the club. Today, they may get 10 or 12, and some will be does. There are very few deer on club property now. In recent years, they have planted some sizeable food plots. There are more bear showing up than deer! The bear just love those turnips that come up in the plots. Some of the club members would go down in the evening just to watch the bears. The odds of getting a bear were better than getting a buck when the season opened.

Changes and Choices

In 1967, Mart was given a promotion and sent down to Cortland as district Forest Ranger. After a couple of years in Cortland, he received a call from the Chairman of Bisby Lodge. He offered Mart the job of managing the Bisby Club. Mart was very flattered with that offer, but currently he was occupying one of the best jobs in the world. He didn't think anyone could convince him to leave. The Chairman lived in Ithaca, not very far from Cortland. He suggested that they have lunch some day and just talk it over.

Long story short, Mart accepted the position. He replaced Floyd Galliger, who had been there for 42 years. At first, he was in charge of giving their people the best vacation possible. This quickly expanded into maintaining the road system and then running the club's forestry program. He was given the title of Resource Manager, where he had charge of everything outside of the Three Lodges. Later he was appointed General Manager of the whole club. Recalling Thad's words earlier, "Mart was very good for the club." He retired from the club after 22 years of service and was only 1 of 3 to be given lifetime membership on the club.

Retirement for Mart means he just changed his work format around. Timber cruising, real estate sales, writing a book ("Adirondack Character"), and also writing a weekly column in *The Adirondack Express* are only a few of his various activities. Mart has been an avid hunter, trapper, and fisherman all his life. I was surprised to learn that he doesn't conform to the expected behavior of a dedicated sportsman. He has almost no photographs. Mart has also taken some fine whitetail trophies in past years. He has no mounts, except one that Nancy wanted of a deer their son had taken. He doesn't hang onto any racks. He gives them all away. His good friend Morgan Roderick took one of his biggest heads and had it mounted for himself. Looking back on his many years in the field, Mart admitted, "There were a few times when I should have had a camera!"

Mart Allen with his best "Dear," Nancy. They are celebrating 57 years together! (Allen family photo)

Close friends for life, L to R: Mart Allen and Morgan Roderick. They grew up in Phoenix, NY, and went through Ranger School together. They shared a real knowledge of common sense skills for working in the woods! (Photo complements of Lynn Roderick)

The Raymond L. Massett Legacy

Almost all Adirondack deer hunters are familiar with the name Massett, especially if you put the name "Jim" in front of it. Jim has been actively hunting the Adirondacks for 63 seasons to date, with well over 100 bucks to his credit. Jim brought a lot of notoriety to the family name when he began giving seminars on how to successfully track big Adirondack bucks. However, there is a lot more deer hunting connected to the family name, aside from Jim's outstanding record. Jim's father, Raymond L. Massett began a hunting legacy back in 1932 that was incredibly successful.

Ray's parents had immigrated from Germany. They bought a small farm on Teal Ave. in Syracuse, NY. Ray was born there in 1910. By 1932, Ray was peddling fresh produce and fruit for Lang & Rose Distributors out of Syracuse. Ray had a route up Route 28 through Old Forge and around the Fulton Chain of Lakes. He sold to stores, large camps, and summer resorts. He met his sweetheart, Agnes Dearcy, in Inlet while she was working at E.W. Edward's summer home. They were married that same year in Inlet at St. Anthony's Church.

Ray had no real background in hunting, but he went deer hunting out of Inlet with some friends that fall. They hunted near Limekiln Lake and he really enjoyed the experience. One time he traveled up to Piseco Lake to hunt. However, it was quite a hassle just to get up there and he couldn't see where the hunting was any better. In the next few years, he grew to love the country just east of Limekiln Lake. When it came to hunting deer, Ray was a natural at deer tracking. Very few clues ever escaped his attention. In time, whenever someone had trouble finding a wounded buck, they would go to Ray for help. With snow on the ground, he would get his buck every fall by tracking it. He used to tell his sons, "Tracking a buck is like turning the pages of a book!" A book Ray truly enjoyed.

Ray began hunting what is now called "The Moose River Plains Wild Forest" when there was just a 2 rut wagon road leading into Kenwell's place on Otter Brook. He hunted out of small remote cabins at first. The Gould Paper Company owned 15,710 acres of property in there. In 1949, they offered hunting groups lease options on blocks of their property. Ray and his group leased 3,500 acres and called it the Mount Tom Club. They were bordered on the north by Bear Pond Club, the east by Lost Brook Club, and the south by Tamarack Club.

The Mount Tom Club quickly filled up with close friends, and many family members. James Hart had married Ray's sister Florence. This marriage produced 11 children, 4 girls and 7 boys. All the boys were hunters. Their oldest boy Ray (called Brud) was Ray Massett's closest friend. In time, they all hunted out of remote Adirondack camps, some a lot longer than others. Ray had 3 boys and one girl; Ray, Jim, Tom, and Irene.

The following chapters will give you an idea of what it was like to hunt with the Massetts and Harts. The people that shared these camps treasure these memories. They count them as some of the very best times in their life. There are many duplicate names and some nick-names. In an effort to eliminate some confusion, I will give you a list of names of family and friends that may appear in these stories.

Name:	AKA:
Family:	
Raymond L. Massett	Kemo (as in Kemo sabe)
Ray Massett Jr.	Ramie
Jim Massett	Butch
Tom Massett	
James Hart Sr.	
James Hart	Jimmy
Ray Hart	Brud
Dick Hart	Dickie
Ken Hart	
Cliff Hart	
Ed Hart	
George Sutton	Pudgy
Bus Sutton	
Roy Hart	
Close friends:	
Mahlon Stone	Stony
Joe Spurchise	
Marty Bergin	
Terry Bostian	
Brian Bostian	

Some of these people have passed on, but there are many left to give testimony. Read on!

Don Hart

In 1937, when he was about 10 years old, Don remembers going into the Red River camp during summer. He remembered the cabin being infested with snakes. Two bunks were up against a wall and there was one window. He saw his father throw a snake out the door, then Don saw one watching him that was laying between the logs. There were others, but it was dark in the cabin. That evening when he went to sleep, he was thinking about snakes. He thought he could feel something on him near his tummy. It was warm in the cabin, so he wasn't wearing much. He felt something move and sat up quickly, banging his head against the spruce pole supports on the top bunk. He threw his belt across the floor, thinking it was a snake! They cooked on the woodstove and had a kerosene lamp. If they needed a bath it was in the Red River! The Gould Paper Company owned the property. In 1947, they started building a serviceable road into their holdings so they could begin logging operations. They were greatly improving the old 2 rut wagon road that Kenwell's used.

"The Red River" in the Moose River Plains Wild Forest. (Don Hart photo)

Red River Cabin. L to R: Sam, Stony, Ray Sr. (Ken Hart photo)

In early March of 1948, Don Hart, Dick Hart, and Joe Spurchise attempted to hike in and do some beaver trapping. Don was just out of the service and his mother saved all the money he sent home, $650.00. He bought a 1939 Dodge with it and they drove up to the gate at Limekiln. At that time, construction on the new road had only progressed ½ mile or so in from the gate. They had planned on walking in, but the snow was crotch deep. They returned to Syracuse and borrowed 2 pair of snowshoes and some skis with rope bindings. Now they hiked all the way in to where the bridge crossed Red River. Their trail in was along the base of 7th Lake Mountain, but traveling up on the frozen river would be easier. After snowshoeing up the river a while, Dickie told Joe (who had a very light pack) to go on ahead to get a fire started in the stove and put on some tea. Joe went on ahead of them.

When Don and Dickie walked up river to the cabin site, they could see Joe up on the bank, kind of squatting down and sitting on the back of his ankles. This was something he did often. Dickie hollered up, "Joe, have you got the tea made?" Joe replied, "Well, I would if I could only find the camp!" Dickie said, "What in the hell are you talking about? The camp is right behind you!" Joe said, "I found the tree with all our traps in it, but no cabin!" They walked up to investigate and, sure enough, the cabin had only recently been burned down. There was an old set of snowshoe tracks heading back down to where a new bridge was started to cross the Red River.

Back out on the road, they walked down to another small cabin. This was called the Halfway Camp. In the earlier days, it was half way in to Kenwell's and used as a place to rest the horses or get in out of the weather. A sign was put out at the bridge because Ray Sr. and Stoney were coming in that night.

When Ray and Stoney arrived, they told them about the cabin. They suspected some locals that had a cabin in the area. They were jealous of Ray's group because his camp was very successful. Now they had to have a new camp. The Halfway Camp was purchased from Gerald Kenwell's son for $50.00 later that year. Just the building, no property.

Don Hart's first buck was a heartbreaker! He was just a young hunter at the time, but he was eager to hunt. It was early in the season and their group was going to push Mitchell Ponds Mountain. Don had a Remington semi-automatic shotgun. He was a real good shot with it and could hit almost anything he shot at. He asked his father if he could walk the logging road out to the gate during the push. The fellows that were doing the push were waiting in what they called "the dugout," on the back side of Mitchell Mountain. At any rate, the push started and Don was taking his time stopping and going along the logging road. He was almost out to the gate when he heard something that sounded like a horse breathing hard. Don turned to look and he saw this big-racked buck heading toward the gate. He shot at it 3 times and he was positive he'd hit it. The buck was really working to make

After improvements were made at the Halfway Camp by Mount Tom. Tom Massett on the front step. (Tom Massett photo)

Removing the snow load from Halfway Cabin roof in late winter. (Tom Massett photo)

forward progress as it went out of site. Don didn't even have a knife with him, so he ran down the road to tell his father. Everyone was there and ready to head for home.

James asked him if the deer went down. The answer of course was no. Don went on to say that the deer looked like it was laboring, but of course a beginner has no credibility. Dickie offered to go back with Don, but Pa said, "No, we only have one car and everybody else wants to leave." So, it was Don's belief that his very first buck, and it was a big one, was wasted because of a rush to get home. That was a heartbreaker for young Don.

The Stinking Buck!

The first time the group camped at Stink Lake Mountain, Don, Marty, and Dickie were together. Marty Bergin and Dickie had hunted off in another direction. Don was up on a small ridge when down the ridge he saw a doe walk out. A short while later another deer came out of the spruce trees. This one had a rack of antlers on it. Don was calm and aimed carefully at the buck. At the shot, the sights had looked good and the buck bolted off. Don was sure the buck had been hit. Before he could thoroughly check for a hit, Marty and Dickie showed up. Then Tom Massett and Ken Hart showed up also. They checked out the area where the buck was and Dickie kept insisting Don missed it. Marty only found one cut hair. Dickie wanted to move on, but Don argued that even though it was a long shot, the buck wouldn't have bolted off like it did if it wasn't hit. Everyone started to leave, but Don stayed and tried to find more evidence of a hit with no results.

Their weather remained warm and in the morning they began hunting the hill across from where Don had shot at the buck. A shot ran out below Don and then he could hear someone shouting, "I found him!" The buck was laying down dead in the brook that ran between the hillsides. It was a real nice buck that dressed 175 lbs with a 8-point rack. Jim Massett had come into camp during the night and attempted to dress it out. This buck had been hit in the shoulder with the bullet tracking into the paunch where it did a lot of damage. When Jim opened it up, the stink made him head for the bushes to heave. Dickie said, "I'll finish the job, he can't be that bad!" Then Dickie started heaving! Eventually the buck was dressed and rinsed out. Don brought the buck to a butcher in Cicero. When he picked it up, the butcher warned him that it might not be any good. Some of it had turned green! When they tried to use it later, it all turned green! The stinking buck from Stink Lake Mountain was tossed!

The Winter Migration

In 1965, late in the season, Ray Hart (Brud) called Don for a late season hunt into the Moose River Plains. So Brud, Don, and his 14 year-old son, Donnie, and Ray Massett (Kemo) went up. Brud had found a real good run on the Moose River Ridge that the deer use when the snow gets deep. He discovered it years earlier. It's a corridor they use to access their deer yards in the plains. The snow was deep now, so they planned on hunting this area.

Don and his son were going to go in and hunt along this corridor. Brud and Kemo would make a wide circle and come in from different angles. When Don got in near the migration trail, it wasn't long before he spotted deer in the distance. He was separated from Donnie by a few yards and Donnie had a better view. The deer came into view slowly and they counted 8 doe. The doe actually came very close to the 2 onlookers when off in the distance where he first spotted the deer, a buck came into view. It had a real nice rack on it and Don was just waiting for the first clear shot. Not long afterward, the buck stepped clear of the trees and Don raised his rifle. Before he could shoot, a shot ran out and then another, making the buck race off.

Brud had spotted the buck in the distance also and decided to shoot even though it was a very long shot. It was a clean miss, so both opportunities were lost.

Don and his son continued to hunt that deer corridor into the plains. They counted 24 deer before the days end, but no more chances at a buck. Kemo got a nice buck over on the Rock Dam Trail later in the day.

Cliff Hart was a professional boxer in the welter weight division. He was a golden glove champion when he fought as an amateur. Anyway, he spent a month hunting up in the woods one year and was in great shape from carrying in all the gear and packing out the bucks. He killed 2 that fall and near the end of the season his brother came in to tell him his manager was trying to reach Cliff as he had a fight lined up for him. Cliff came out, took the fight and knocked out his opponent. Then back up to the woods for the remainder.

Don also was a professional boxer, but did not have as many fights as Cliff. Ray (Brud) also fought and was good at it.

Ray Hart

Raymond Hart (Brud) was the 2nd oldest child in the Hart family. Brud was very close to Ray Massett (Kemo). Like Kemo, when snow was on the ground, he would be tracking his bucks. He was very successful at it also! In the early years, especially being part of a big family, meat was greatly appreciated, and never wasted.

Brud was married in 1942 with the understanding that he would soon enlist in the war effort. He joined the army later that year. After basic training and 2 weeks in intelligence school, he was sent to Ft. Bragg, NC. He had signed up to be a paratrooper and his training began here. When school started it wasn't long before he had his first airplane ride and parachute jump together. Training completed, he was assigned to company "H" and was part of the 82nd Air Borne division. There were 27 training jumps before his first combat jump.

Into the War

On July 9th of 1943 Brud did his first combat jump into Sicily. He was the acting platoon sergeant at the time. Brud sailed down through bursts of anti-aircraft fire (ack-ack fire), and small arms fire. He landed hard, but safe in a grove of olive trees. Their mission was to help secure "Biazzi Ridge." They moved up to the higher ground where some heavy fighting was going on. Brud said, "The firing was intense! The bullets were cracking and whistling all around us!" Two men were hit right in front of him. They were just digging in near the top when 9 or 10 Germans with machine guns came running up the hill towards them. Brud's troopers saw them first, and cut loose with everything they had. Three were killed, serveral wounded, and the rest captured.

Reinforcement troopers were expected to come in that evening on a fleet of low flying C-47s. Through a horrible lack of communication between the paratroop commanders and the naval officers, our Navy shot down most of the C-47s as they passed over heading for the drop zone. Twenty three aircraft loaded with our guys went down in flames. Only 555 men of a 2,304 man combat team were accounted for 24 hours after the disaster. When the mistake was discovered, men cried like babies and moral was down near zero!

Later in the campaign on August 27th, Brud's shooting skills made headlines. His platoon was moving in on a German stronghold. From behind some buildings, Brud could see a German officer escaping on a motorcycle. He shot him right off the speeding bike, even though it was a long, difficult shot. The officer was carrying a briefcase full of important documents. Some of Brud's fellow troopers who had witnessed the event gave the story to a war correspondent without him knowing it. The story was published in *"Yank Magazine," "Stars and Stripes"* and even made his hometown Syracuse newspaper.

Jumping into Hell

Other combat jumps were made at Salerno, Normandy, and Holland. Normandy was the worst! Many years ago Brud told a brief account of his D-Day jump into Normandy. He was on one of many planes after dark heading for Normandy on the 5th of June 1944. D-Day was on the 6th. Here is his story.

"I was on a plane, and just before midnight we jumped. A lot of parachutes, and a lot of ack-ack fire, tracers, and explosions, everything! The whole place lights up like a circus! In fact, the machine gun nest that I landed near, fired several bursts at me as I came down. I could see the tracers coming and they look like they are floating, just floating. Then all of a sudden RAP, CRACK, CRACK, they go by you. You have a helpless feeling as you float downwards.

"I landed pretty hard. I was stunned. I landed on my back and flat, and as I lay there gathering my senses the Germans fired several bursts at me. My first thought was to get the only weapon available to me at the moment. I had a .45 tied to my leg with a piece of rawhide. I slid that out, and as I did two German soldiers came over, they were probably going to check me out and probably shoot me. I shot the closest one first, and then the second one threw a (potato masher) grenade over me. It's a good thing it was a concussion grenade, instead of a fragmentation grenade! If it had been a fragmentation grenade, then I would have been a goner. I was covered with powder burns. It knocked me for a loop. I don't know how long I was out, but they had dragged me into their corner of the woods.

"When I woke up they were trying to question me. Of course I couldn't hear a thing, but I knew they were trying to question me. I was bleeding from both ears, and I thought I was dead, and they must have too! They picked up and left me there. I crawled until about 4 PM the next afternoon towards Sainte Mere Eglise, which wasn't that far. That was our objective, to take the main roads going into Sainte Mere Eglise.

"I came out on the main road and spotted a couple of our boys. They were only a couple hundred yards from the stone farmhouse where they had set up an aid station. I stayed there overnight, the next morning they sent me out to a landing craft lined up with Germans and our boys. I wound up in the hospital for 6 or 7 weeks. When I got out, the CO told me I didn't have to jump into Holland, but I figured my cousin, Bob Sutton, had just been killed before that, so I decided to go and make the jump. It was the easiest one of the four!"

Ray went on to serve until the end of the war. He was discharged from Fort Dix, NJ on July 8th, 1945. He was awarded the Purple Heart, the Silver Star, and the Bronze Star along with other decorations. He took a great deal of pride in his Paratrooper Medal which carried 4 stars, one for each combat jump he made! Ray passed on to our Lord on August 12, 1999. Many people, especially today, have no idea of what our war veterans have gone through. Be sure to show respect to our men and women in uniform.

"Bath and Lodging – 25 Dollars"

One spring, Brud and his wife Barbara decided to take a canoe trip from the south branch of the Moose River, starting at the Moose River Plains, ten miles in from Limekiln Lake and canoe down to the bridge on Route 28 at McKeever. They left a car at McKeever and then drove into the Plains where they launched the canoe. Late on the second day, while crossing the Adirondack League Club lands, they tipped over in the cold water. Nearby was one of the Club's cabins, so they went back to it and built a fire to dry out and spent the night. Early the next morning, they heard a vehicle come in. A group lead by Mart Allen came in to fish and they were discovered. Mart had to report the incident to the Club President, N. Baker, who insisted that Hart be charged with trespassing on private lands. Mart did not want to do this, but as he was in the employ of the Club, he had no choice. Ray decided to plead innocent and a date was set for the trial. One of the members that Mart was guiding was a retired Admiral of the US Navy. When Mart told the Admiral that Ray Hart was a war hero who had made four combat jumps as a paratrooper and had been wounded on D-Day, he said, "Gee, I wish I had known that. I would have called him my guest." I believe the fee for a guest then was around $40.00 per day. Ray went up to the trial and pleaded his case, explaining how they tipped the canoe over, etc. The judge found him guilty with a fine of $25.00. Cheaper than being treated as a guest!

Raymond Massett Jr.

Ray "Ramie" took his first trip into camp at 9 years of age. He didn't actually start hunting until he turned 14. On that first hunt, he carried a 16 ga. Remington shotgun and just followed his father around. He saw deer, but nothing with antlers. During these early years of the 30s and 40s, the Old Military Road from the War of 1812 could still be found. It was cut right across the plains and was quite visible in some areas.

Ramie got his first buck the following year with a Model 8 .32 caliber Remington. He was hunting ahead of his father on the trail into Beaver Lake. Ramie spotted a deer up on a small hardwood ridge and it was a spike horn. He hit it hard with his 1st shot and a 2nd shot put it down. His father also killed a spike horn later that day. They dragged both bucks out to the road. From there it was on a 2-wheeled tubular-framed deer cart to the gate.

Ray Massett with his father and 2 spike horns. Far right, Bus Sutton. 1948

1947, 13 bucks for 13 hunters – This photo appeared in the "Syracuse Herald Journal." Photo taken at their Teal Ave. home in Syracuse. (Don Hart photo)

The Red River Buck

Ramie's first big buck came while hunting out of the Halfway Camp. Ramie and Ray Sr. got back to camp late one afternoon when the whole crew was out hunting. Ray did most of the cooking so he went about getting things started. He looked at Ramie and said, "Don't quit hunting now, this is the bewitching hour!" Ramie replied, "What do you mean?" "It's the last hour before full dark and now is when the bucks start to move!"

Donald's brother (Brud) had seen a big buck and its signs along the Red River. Everyone knew it was there, but so far nobody had a crack at him. Ramie left camp with his .351 Winchester. It was a lousy deer cartridge, but that's what he carried that year. He knew of the big buck also. With less than an hour to hunt, he walked the wagon road over to the bridge that crossed Red River. There was a steep bank going down to the river and when he looked across, there standing in the scrub brush along the river and about 90 yards off, was this big rocker of a buck. Ramie brought his rifle up and fired. The buck just stood there. He drew down a fine bead on the buck and shot again. This time the buck wheeled and ran off. He fired once more as it ran. Ramie was still a very young hunter and had no experience in tracking. He walked right back to the cabin and told his father, "Pa, I just wounded a big buck!" Ray Sr. replied, "No kidding." He didn't stop cooking or even look at Ramie. Ramie told him what went down, so Ray shut everything down and grabbed his rifle.

They walked down to the bridge and Ray asked him just where exactly he shot from and where was the buck when he shot. Ramie guided him over to where the buck was and Ray found blood. Ray told him to stay put and he began tracking the buck. It was dry and there was no snow cover. There was a small ridge across the river and Ramie watched his father go up and over it. Suddenly, he heard 2 shots ring out. Ray downed the buck when it jumped from its bed. Ramie walked in and his father congratulated him on getting a really big buck.

After admiring it a little more, Ray said, "It's getting near dark, I better get this guy dressed out!" Just as he was about to grab the buck, it suddenly came back to life and tried to gore Ray with its antlers. A quick shot in the neck ended it all for sure. This buck weighed at 205 lbs dressed and the oversized rack carried 12 points. Not bad for a 16 year old hunter! Everyone called it the "Red River Buck."

Air Freight

When Ramie was around 15 years old, his father wanted Scotty Windhousen to fly some freight back into a lake near their hunting area. The supplies included a huge army tent. Even though it was rolled up tight, it was too big to put inside, so Scotty lashed it to one of the floats. Scotty and Don sat up front; Stoney and young Ramie were in the back with all the freight. The aircraft roared off down the lake and soon became airborne. This was Ramie's first flight, but he noticed that the plane never flew level, but remained tipped to one side. The whole aircraft started shaking and Scotty made a quick circle to set the plane back down at his base. He said, "Sorry boys, but that tent won't be flying in with me!" The tent rode in on a deer cart and with a great deal of difficulty.

The loggers always treated their bunch of hunters well. The cooks, Oscar and Homer, would treat them to coffee, milk, donuts, or pie. Sometimes, they would stop and offer them a ride back toward their camp. The logging boss was named Pennard and he was from Long Lake. Most of the loggers were French men. They spoke with broken English. Ramie was walking out to the gate one day and still had 3 miles to go when a truck stopped by him. The driver offered him a lift so Ramie got in. Ramie initiated the conversation by asking, "Who do you work for, Pennard?" The driver shot back, "I are Pennard!" His logging camp was about 7 miles in.

Crunch, Crunch

When Ramie was 22, he and his brother Tom got laid-off from their jobs early and just before deer season. They were camped in near Benedict Creek that year. One week the weather had been wet and then quickly got sharply colder. The leaves under the trees were all frozen down. In the swamps and beaver meadows, the pools of high water had froze over and then the water receded rapidly. This left many areas of thin shell ice covering the ground. Ramie was hunting along a logging road toward Mitchell Ponds. There was an inactive beaver meadow off to his right. Every once in a while, he could hear a faint "crunch, crunch" off in the meadow. He was crunching too, on frozen puddles and dirt raised by the frost. The "crunch, crunch" in the meadow continued every so often and he would get up on a dirt bank or whatever to see if he could spot the source. Finally this buck stepped into view way down the meadow. Ramie shot twice at the buck, hitting it both times. It died in the meadow. It was a real nice 8-point.

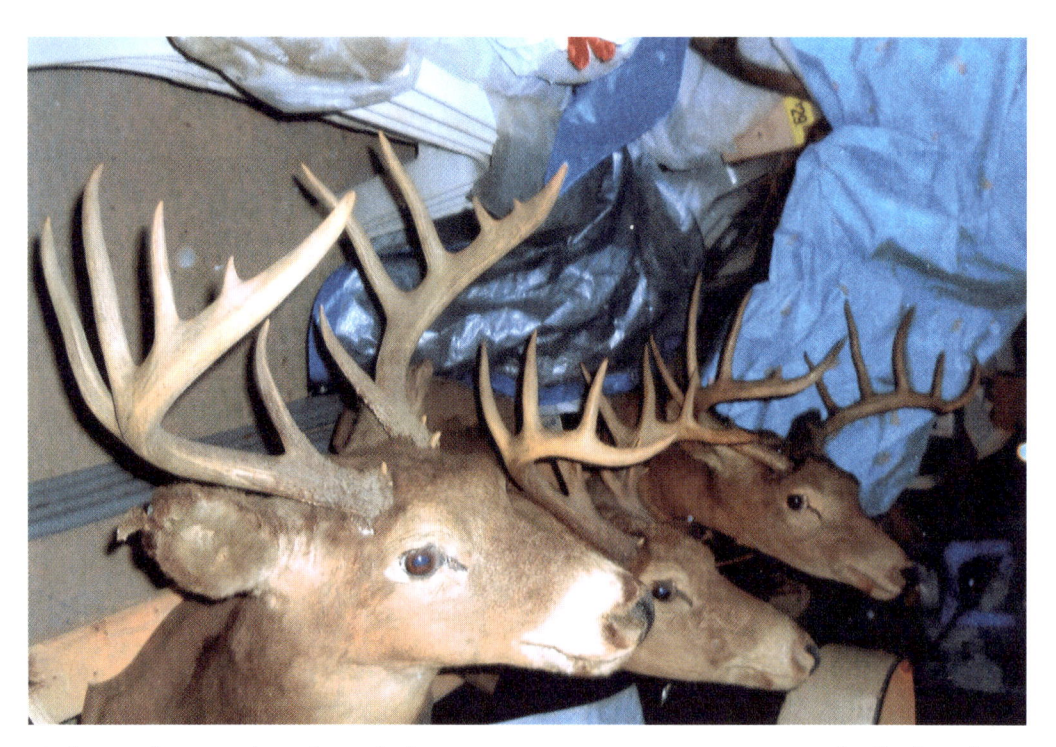

A few good mounts from the early days. In storage at Ramie Massett's. (Bob Elinskas photo)

Ramie Massett with the crunch, crunch buck. (Ray Massett photo)

Jim Massett

Jim would go up to deer camp on summer vacations as a young lad. Then in 1950, his father brought him along on a hunt. During that hunt, he was right behind his father when he saw him raise his rifle. Jim saw the buck fall, but never saw it before the shot. It was a beautiful 10-pointer. The following year, 1951, he was in the woods with his own rifle and looking for another 10-pointer.

Jim remembers the '50s and '60s as being the best ever for hunting the Adirondacks. All of their guys would take the same week off in November, so there would be 10-12 guys in camp every night. They all hunted hard and wouldn't quit until dark every day. It was always a good time, listening to each man's adventures for the day. With a lot of deer in the woods, they saw a lot of action.

A young Jim Massett with his father out at the Limekiln Trail Head. He watched his Pa take this buck. (Ken Hart photo)

L to R: Bus Sutton, Ramie, Stony, Kemo (Ray Sr.), Don Hart & Jim Massett.

The Trophy Hunter

Jim didn't start passing up smaller bucks until the early 1960s. That's when he realized he was capable of putting a mature Adirondack buck on the ground every fall. There were decent numbers of mature bucks to hunt every fall until the mid to late 1980s. That is also when the coyote population in the mountains began to balloon. Starting in early winter, coyotes would often hunt in packs. They seemed to know that a rut weary buck was now an easy target. The older mature buck was becoming a scarce item. They were still there in reduced numbers, but it was taking quite a lot longer to locate a track you wanted to follow.

Any mature Adirondack whitetail is a real trophy. Our mountain deer are the foxiest bucks on the planet. Many of today's dedicated whitetail hunters have hunted deer from Texas to Saskatchewan and Montana to New Brunswick. They all agree, you won't find a tougher buck than our Adirondack whitetail.

They tented in many areas – Horn Lake, Red River, Indian River, 2-mile Brook, and Natural Hatchery Brook. Over the years, they hunted most of the Moose River Plains at one time or another. In those days, Jim was in top physical condition. He loved to run and could put some miles behind him if he had to. He read in Larry Benoit's book how he would sometimes run on the track of a buck, (in later years, Larry told Jim that he never ran after a buck). Jim would sometimes run a track. He would often start a buck 8 or 9 times while jogging after it.

One day he got on the track of a real big buck. During the day, it led him across a section of the Adirondack League Club (you hate to quit on a big one when you have 3 or 4 miles invested in him). Eventually, the track let him off the club property and over to Golden Stair Mountain. Since the buck was cruising, Jim began running on its track. The track turned sharply downhill at one point, so Jim stopped to look over the woods ahead. Then he noticed another hunter below him. He waved at him, but the guy didn't wave back. This man started toward Jim. Jim didn't really know if he was on some posted, leased property or what, but he did not want any confrontation. He was about 9 miles from his tent camp, so he turned and started jogging back to camp. He was thinking, "If that guy wants to talk to me bad enough, he can follow my tracks all the way to camp!" Jim considers the Moose River Plains "home." He has hunted it, even if only a day or two, every year since his first hunt in 1951.

There was another buck Jim trailed in deep snow for most of a day. When he finally jumped him, he was with a doe. He didn't have a shot so he ran as fast as he could after the buck. How fast can you run in a foot or more of snow? After a good sprint, he came to a windfall the buck had jumped over, but Jim couldn't. Going around the end of this blow-down, Jim looked down the hill and there stood the buck. Jim was breathing real heavy from running and thought, "It's going to be a miracle shot if can hit him!" Boom! He took him right through the shoulders and dropped him. He dressed him out real quick and by then, it was 4:30 PM. He was 5 miles in from the truck and he told Tom (his brother) that he would meet him at 5 PM. Tom guessed what happened and had a nice warm fire going while he waited.

Antler Tracks

In 1970, the Massett group was hunting out of a camp that was 6 ½ miles back in the Plains. It was Sunday and Jim was walking back to camp from church in Inlet. He had a small back pack on and was carrying his rifle. About 4 miles in, he walked into the woods to get a drink from a small brook. There was snow cover and right by the brook, were the tracks of a big buck. Jim loaded his rifle and began to track that buck. This buck came to a fallen tree with mushrooms growing out of the trunk. The buck began feeding on these mushrooms, so he reached and rolled his head for the lowest ones and his rack would leave an impression in the snow. He counted 4 tines on one side and 4 on the other. Any brow tines would be unlikely to show. He didn't get this buck, but always afterwards, he would look for signs in the snow of a rack. When a buck puts his nose straight down into the snow for ferns or beechnuts, you can get a good idea of how wide and high his antlers are. The widest spread Jim ever saw was close to 26 inches. That was up on Indian Lake Mountain. He went back 3 or 4 times looking just for that buck, but never could connect.

Jim likes the .308 cartridge to hunt with. It's the same bullet weight choices as a 30-06 and travels only slightly slower. It's a shorter cartridge, so the rifle action has less distance to travel. He believes this also lessens the chance of a malfunction. Jim hunted with a 44 magnum for several years, but considers it a little too light for the variety of shots he has to make. Jim's first rifle was a .32 Remington that his father bought for him. His older brother, Ray, had a .351 Winchester. Jim liked the Winchester better so he swapped rifles and killed his first buck in 1951 with that Winchester. Ray went into the service in 1952, so he hunted with Ray's rifle, the Remington, while he was away. He took several bucks with it and came to like it more than the Winchester. His father bought another .32 Remington and gave it to Jim.

A Good Day on Mitchell Ponds Ridge

In 1955, Jim was up on Mitchell Ponds Ridge with his .32 Remington. His father was also in the same general area. Around mid-morning, he heard Ray shoot. Ray was much higher on the ridge than Jim, so he started hunting up towards Ray to see if he connected. On the way up, Ray shot 2 more times. It was all over when Jim got there. Ray had a big buck down with a beautiful rack of antlers. It had a wide spread with 9 long tines. Jim said, "Nice buck, Pa! Nine points!" Ray said, "No, it's 10!" Then Jim picked the rack up and counted 9 points. Then Ray said, "Oh, yes. Well, it's a 9 then."

Seeing that big buck got Jim all enthused about hunting again. After leaving his father and the buck, he continued hunting along, but extra slow. He hadn't gone 200 yards when he saw a black bear coming up the ridge. He killed that bear and it was a big one. Jim guessed it at 400 pounds. It was his first bear. He was so excited, he streaked back to tell his father. This was one of the first years Ray was guiding, so he had a crew bring it out whole. It hung for a while in a tree. This area was also currently being logged. All the loggers knew where the bear was hanging. They would occasionally stop and rub some of the bear fat on their LL Bean leather uppers.

You're Not Going Anywhere

On the south side of Mount Tom, there is a steep grade of ledges. From above this ledge, you can get an unobstructed view of Mitchell Ponds Ridge and the Plains area off to the east. Jim enjoyed a little down time there early in the season, just to relax and take in the view. He was taking in the view one fall and enjoying the solitude when suddenly the peace and serenity was shattered from across the valley on Mitchell Ridge. Ba-boom, ba-boom, ba-boom! Three shots echoed across the hardwoods. Jim was thinking it might be his older brother Ray. Then 3 more shots rang out. After a few minutes of silence, 2 more shots. A few more minutes and

L to R: Mahlon Stone, Bob LaMountain & Mike Benoffski. This was a small cabin that they occasionally used up on Mount Tom in the 1940s. One of their hunters filled the stove with wood one morning, but forgot to damper it down. On returning from the hunt, they saw where their cabin had burned to the ground. (Massett photo)

another shot. Then he heard someone shout, "Ba blah, ba blah, ba blah!" He couldn't make out what was said and even wondered if a drive was getting underway.

Back in camp that evening, he found out it was his brother Ramie that was doing all the shooting. He jumped a buck over on the ridge and managed to hit it in a hind quarter on the first volley. He kept jumping the buck as he followed it down the ridge, but wasn't able to anchor it with a killing shot. He was getting a little frustrated with all his shooting, until he finally hit it solid and dropped the buck. Jim asked him what the shouting was all about. Ramie smiled and said, "when I finally walked down to him, I hollered, 'You're not going anywhere, you S.O.B.!'"

Jim told me that back in these days you had a pretty good idea of just where their crew was going to be hunting each day. They also knew what everyone was shooting and could guess pretty close by the sound of the shots who was doing the shooting.

The Massett's carried many of their bucks out of the woods backpack style. The front legs of the deer are either tied inside or outside the hind legs depending on the deer's size. On a small deer, the front legs would be tied outside the rear leg at the hocks. On a big deer you would tie them inside the rear legs and tied them where they felt comfortable. They would sometimes put a rain coat between the packer's back and the deer to keep the blood at bay. Jim packed a lot of bucks out. They would at times, call him "The Workhorse."

54 *In the Woods with* **Adirondack Sportsmen**

Mitchell Ponds with the Moose River Plains beyond. Little Moose Mountain is top center. (Photo by Bob Elinskas)

Jammed!

While hunting out of their camp on Natural Hatchery Brook, Jim killed a big bodied buck with a 9-point rack. This buck weighed 198 lbs., clean dressed and minus its tenderloins. Ray Sr., Jim, Tom, cousin Alan, and Dick Jones were there for the carry out. Jim was carrying the deer on his back as they bushwhacked back out to camp. In one area he came up to two windfalls that he had to cross. They were laying parallel to one another, but the closer one was a little lower than the next one. Jim sat his butt down on the log and then lifted one leg over. When he lifted his other leg, he went right over backwards between the 2 windfalls. The legs of the buck were jammed up against the bottom of the first windfall. Jim couldn't move and he couldn't get out! Meanwhile, since he didn't get hurt, everyone was having a good laugh at his expense. They finally broke a few branches on the second windfall, reached in and grabbed the buck by his antlers and pulled both buck and packer (still attached) out on the far side.

By Compass

More recently in 2003, Jim killed a real big 10-pointer off in the Hills, near Raquette Lake. He had been after this same buck for 2 years and now it was down, dead and his. There was snow on the ground, but the weather had warmed up and it was now raining. Since it was late afternoon, he didn't think there would be any snow left by the next day. He looked around for landmarks and then followed a compass line out to the road. Jim called up 2 of his friends, Roger Cronizer and Joe DiNitto, to give him a hand in bringing out the buck. They came up the next morning and by that time, all the snow was gone.

Jim led the guys back into the hills using his reverse compass line. Of course, everything looks different with the snow off. He got back into the area where he thought he killed the buck, but he had hidden it. Joe gave him hell for hiding it. It took him a good half an hour to locate his buck. With a GPS, it would have been so easy! Jim still doesn't use one. His buddies turned out to be really "good" buddies. They dragged the buck all the way out to the road and even loaded it into his truck for him. That's good!

Jim's Biggest Buck

Jim had been tracking a big buck for 3 ½ to 4 hours. By mid-afternoon, he was up on a big hillside of mixed hardwood and spruce cover. He stopped and was looking over the cover ahead when a doe ran down the slope in front of him. Only

Jim was a strong deer packer! In his prime he was AKA "The Workhorse."
(Massett photo)

seconds later, a buck ran down the hill after her. Jim had his rifle up, but not quick enough for that first good chance. The buck stopped down the slope, but 2 big tree trunks hid its body. The buck started running again, but totally unaware of Jim's presence. Jim ran down the hill after the buck. When he got down on his tracks, he could see where 2 deer were running. He didn't want to stay on the tracks now, so he veered to his right, above the line of the tracks. There was a logging road along the base of the hill. Jim didn't think they would cross the road, so he continued on looking even more to his right. He came across their tracks again and it appeared they were heading for the top of the hill. Jim went up after them and stood watching near the summit. The tracks indicated they had run down the other side towards Governor's Brook. He stayed put and watched a while longer. Then he heard, "blaat, blaat." In the distance, he can see this doe moving slow and just taking one step at a time. He was trying to get a better view of her, but the snow was crunchy. A big log lay just ahead, so he moved slowly up to that. It looked like the doe was walking back into the thick spruce trees. Jim then made 3 or 4 grunts from his grunt call. The doe turned and started coming his way. It was then that he saw another deer closing with the doe. Jim had his rifle ready as the deer, screened by limbs and trees, moved closer. Finally, he saw an antler. Then as it moved between 2 trees, he had a clear shot at the neck. Boom! At the shot, the buck disappears. Jim stays at the ready and the doe stays put, even after the shot. Then Jim hears a loud, "clack, clack, clack!" And again, the same sound. Is the buck rubbing his antlers on a tree? Finally it stopped and Jim thought, "I've got to go over there and see what happened!"

Jim walked right by the doe and over to where the buck was hit. What happened was the buck was struck in the neck and the bullet traveled over into a section of its back. That paralyzed its back legs. The buck slid down a bank and the rack got caught up in a spruce pole that was bent over. Every time the buck would struggle to free its rack, the pole would beat against a nearby tree. That was the clacking noise he heard. This buck dressed out at 167 and carried his biggest rack. This was in November of 1992. The 10-point rack later officially scored 152-6 and is currently listed in the New York State Whitetail Record Book.

Jim presented his first Adirondack Deer Hunting seminar in 1977 at Finger Lakes Community College. He has given no less than one and often several seminars in each of the last 37 years. His younger brother, Tom, would sometimes contribute to these seminars. Then about 15 years ago, Joe DiNitto from Marcy, NY, joined the presentations. Joe is an exceptional deer tracker, with an ongoing success record that is hard to beat. His down to earth, easy to understand analysis of the deer tracking process brought a whole new energy to the shows. Jim thought Joe was the best thing that could have happened for the seminars.

At 76, Jim is winding down after so many successful seasons in the Adirondacks. He worked hard for his accomplishments. They certainly weren't given to him. His years in the woods spanned from some of the best whitetail hunting the mountains ever experienced to some of the toughest. He still hunts those wild and beautiful Adirondacks. If there is any snow cover, he will be on a track or looking for one. Be sure to say, "Hello!" to him at his next seminar!

Jim with another outstanding Adirondack buck.

L to R: Joe DiNitto & Jim Massett presenting one of many deer hunting seminars. (Photo by Ladd Hale)

Tom Massett

Tom Massett at age 73 is the youngest of the brothers. He began hunting the Adirondacks with his family in 1955, at 15 years of age. He shot his first Adirondack buck in 1956. He was extra glad to take this 7-pointer, because only an hour earlier he missed a different buck. He was worried that back at camp they might cut off his shirt tail for missing a buck! Since 1956, the bucks have fallen regularly to his rifle for over 57 seasons.

The Long Walk to Church

From 1955 to 1960, Ray Massett and Ray Hart started a guiding service in the Moose River Plains. Their camp was 8 ½ miles into the plains from the parking area at Limekiln Lake. Ray Massett was a strict Roman Catholic. Guiding or hunting was no excuse to miss Sunday morning mass. Every Sunday, they would walk the 8 ½ miles out for church at St. Anthony's in Inlet and after mass, back in. The boys, Ray, Jim, and Tom remembered this well. They didn't dare miss mass or they would get their butts kicked!

One Saturday evening they received 4 inches of new snow and Sunday morning looked like the perfect hunting day. Tom's brothers, Ray and Jim, had already left for church. His cousin Ray was telling him, "Tom, it's such a good day to hunt, new snow and all. Why don't you stay and hunt?" Tom gave in and went hunting. He had just crossed the Red River when he started feeling guilty. He turned back and headed out to the road so he could walk to church. However, before he made it to the road, Tom came onto a smoking hot buck track. He only tracked it 50 yards and out jumped the buck. He shot it, opened it up, and tied his tag to the head. Then he streaked for church. He got out to the parking lot at Limekiln Lake and his father and brothers were just returning from mass. Ray started chewing Tom out for missing services. Tom cut in, telling him he could still make 11 o'clock mass in Big Moose. Also, the fact that he had taken his buck that morning took a lot of sting out of his father's reprimand!

Always Carry Cough Drops

In 1962, on opening weekend, they had 5 inches of snow up on the mountain tops. One real nice 8-pointer was already hanging at the Massett camp. In the morning before going out to hunt, Tom told his father, "You know I've never taken a buck up on Mitchell Ponds Mountain. I think I'll go up there today and see if I can find one." Ray answered, "If I was 10 years younger Tom, I'd go up there with you. I'll see you back at camp this evening."

Tom made the hike up into the higher elevations where the snow cover was good. He found an old track that appeared to be a buck and followed it. After only a short distance, he saw where the deer had bedded and now he had a fresh track. He was near a saddle on the mountain, so when he looked down into it, he saw his father. He thought, "Well, look at that. Dad just lost 10 years!"

He walked down to him and said, "Pa, I'm on a fresh buck track. Why don't you go over there and watch and I'll go move the buck." Tom went back on the track. The buck made a loop and hit Tom's track. The deer then ran off toward Ray. Tom is on the track and it is heading right to Ray. Then in the distance, Tom heard his father cough. Then he heard him cough again. Tom is thinking, "This isn't good!" Tom is looking all around. He takes 2 more steps and spots the buck off to his left looking right at him. One quick shot anchored the buck. It should have been Ray's buck, but that nagging cough gave him away.

Fun In The Woods

Everyone in camp was a target when it came to the trickery and jokes. If you spotted one of your buddies hunting along and he was unaware of your presence, you might blow like a deer or grunt like a buck and watch him go on "full alert."

At the old "Halfway Camp" that used to be Kenwell's, they had a water hose that ran from a fresh water stream down to a small foot bridge that crossed a boggy area on a beaver flow. Late one day, Tom's cousin saw Marty Bergin coming down the trail towards the foot bridge. His cousin hid in the spruce trees to scare Marty. The hose was streaming fresh cold water out ¾ of the way across the foot bridge. Marty stopped for a drink of water, then started up and went back for 2 more drinks. Finally he crossed into the spruces and Tom's cousin, laying low, grabbed him by the ankle and growled. Marty let out a loud, "Owwee!!" It scared the hell out of him!

Kenny Heart was up on the side of a mountain in the hardwoods in early fall. The day was warm and it was really breezy. He looked down from his position and could see one of his buddies, Joe Spurchies, sitting with his back against a big tree. Ken thought, "With the wind blowing the leaves around, I wonder how close I can get to him?" He walked right up to him! Joe was sound asleep against that tree, so Ken grabbed Joe's rifle and moved back about 40 yards to watch. About 20 minutes later, Joe sat up, stretched, and started looking around. Then he started looking for his rifle and couldn't find it. Kenny could see Joe pawing through all the nearby leaves and he started laughing out loud! Joe was thinking, "The angels don't want me to hunt anymore!" He couldn't imagine how his rifle could have disappeared.

Deer Signs?

A lot of Gould Paper property was leased out to hunting clubs. Ray's group belonged to the Mount Tom Club. One afternoon, Ray Sr. came down off from Mount Tom to a logging road. There were a couple of fellas tent camping along the road and were in camp. Ray talked with them and learned they had just come down from Mitchell Ponds Ridge. Ray then asked them if they had seen any signs (deer sign) on the ridge. They replied, "Signs? What kind of signs? We didn't see any signs!" Ray walked away thinking, "What did they expect to see? A poster saying, "Deer are in this area!"?

How Are We Doing, Sarge?

Gould required all the lease holders to post their property. On one occasion, Ray Heart was leading their group back out to the Seventh Lake parking area. The doe season was open, so a lot of hunters were trying to fill their tags. They still had 2 miles to go when they met a group coming in. They stopped briefly to talk and Ray asked them where they were going. One of them replied, "We are going in a little further to hunt." Ray said, "It's posted on both sides of the road for 8 miles!" They replied, "Yes, we know, but we have permission to hunt." Ray said, "Really? I'm in the Mount Tom Club. Who gave you permission?" They said, "Uh… Ray Heart gave us permission." To which Ray replied, "I'm Ray Heart!" The guy looked back and said, "How are we doing, Sarge?"

The Mount Tom Club had a mutually beneficial agreement with their neighboring clubs. They could hunt across any of the bordering clubs and they could hunt theirs. It worked well and was almost like hunting in the old days.

The guiding camp by the half way creek was getting too small for their group by 1959. They tore it down and built a bigger 24' x 24' building just across the creek from the old site. Unfortunately, they only had one year to use it. No one had been warned of the coming purchase of Gould property in the Moose River

*There was no warning! The new Halfway Camp in 1959.
They got to use it one season before the State bought out Gould Paper Co.
It was burned down one year later. (Ken Hart photo)*

Jim & Tom with a couple of Moose River Plains buck at Inlet.

Their Indian River gang. L to R: Al VanAuken, Tom Massett, Fred Hanley, Walt Loerzel, Dick Jones, front: Terry Bostian. (Tom Massett photo)

Bringing out a buck the easy way. 1976 Indian River area. Front of bike, Tom Massett, rear, Al VanAuken, red pack, Dick Jones & rear, Fred Hanley. (Tom Massett photo)

64   *In the Woods with* **Adirondack Sportsmen**

Tom Massett with a buck taken on Ice Cave Mt. 1976 (Tom Massett photo)

Indian Lake Mt. buck taken by Al VanAuken. (Tom Massett photo)

A big buck with a freak left side rack. The buck was taken by Tom in 1992 near Big Moose and the rack carried 10 points. (Tom Massett photo)

Plains. Losing their cabin to the state, and also the leasing agreements, was a huge blow to their group. Life goes on though. The deer hunting was still there, so they began using tents. This marked the beginning of many camping locations throughout the Moose River Plains.

Thanksgiving Weekend, 1985

Tom was hunting some leased property in November up on Moynihan Mountain, between upper and lower Moose Ponds and Cedarlands Boy Scout Camp. Up in the spruce trees, near the top, he came across a couple of decent sized deer tracks in the snow. He followed them for a while, but when they headed down the other side, towards McRorie Lake, he left them. He continued on, staying high. The ridge line kind of split on the west end, so he thought he would stop for a while and maybe say a decade or two on his Rosary. Sounds from the much lower elevations, near the Boy Scout Camp, indicated a drive was getting underway. Tom began looking around. Suddenly his eyes focused on a deer about 100 yards away. It was a reddish-brown color and he could see most of its body, but not its head. "God, that looks like a buck!" he thought. It was a good, big deer, but it had its head in the evergreens. He turned his scope up to 9 power and looked again. Tom brought his gun down and then the deer was gone.

He knew that the deer didn't wind him, so he walked over and started tracking it. The deer took him around in a loop and it came to Tom's track. Then it started following those tracks until he came to a place where Tom had urinated. The deer took off running down one ridge, up another, then downhill again. Tom thought, "I'll never catch up to him this way." Finally, the deer slowed to a walk and Tom now figured to try to make a swing on the deer to get ahead of it. He made a big swing and then climbed up on a sizeable rock where he could look down the ridge. As soon as he straightened up on that rock, he could see a deer bounding up the ridge toward him. It was a doe. He now thought, "Something scared that doe. Just sit tight." Meanwhile, the doe decided to bed down about 100 yards off. Tom waited for 10 to 15 minutes and then ate his lunch. A half hour passed and he thought, "Well, there is no buck coming on her track." Tom bleated at her 2 or 3 times, the doe stood up, got a little nervous, then ran back down the slope. She couldn't wind Tom.

Tom back-tracked the doe and saw where his deer had come through and scared her up to where she had bedded. Tom got back on his original track and

Thanksgiving weekend 1985 and the buck Tom tracked for 7 hours. (Massett family photo)

followed it to the base of Buck Mountain, and then towards Long Lake. Now the wind was right on Tom's back and he knows his chances are slim to none of catching this deer. He followed on anyway and the tracks started moving back west near some large rock formations. Tom thought these may have swirled the wind currents around in his favor. He was moving along slowly on the track when he heard a deer blow. About 60 yards ahead, he saw a buck running down the hill broadside. He got 3 shots off before he hit him. That slowed him down enough to finish him off with a neck shot. Tom walked up to a beautiful 11-point buck. He had been on the track since 9 AM and it was then 4 PM.

He dressed out the buck and had it down to a trail on the lower elevations by sundown. It was back to camp in the dark and later that evening, Al VanAuken, George Knoop, and Tom brought him back to camp with a deer cart. The buck later officially scored 139.

Dribble Dribble, Squirt Squirt

Terry Bostian was a fellow deer hunter and a good friend of the Massett's. They would often hunt together out of their various deer camps. On one occasion, Terry had a small camp set up near the base of Ice Cave Mountain. He invited Tom and his father in for a hunt. This was in Ray's later years, when they agreed to go in for a couple days.

Tom and Ray made the hike into his camp and Terry was delighted to see them. Terry's camp wasn't any commercially made tent. It was constructed of a metal pole frame and covered with polyethylene sheeting. There was a cooking and heating area and sleeping area with limited floor space. It was not a spacious shelter.

There were 2 cots set up parallel in the sleeping area with about 2 feet of space in between. When it came time to sack out that evening, Tom volunteered to sleep on the floor between the 2 cots. Terry would have none of that, insisting, "You are my guests and you will have both cots." Then Ray spoke up and said, "What about my pee can? You know I can't make it through the night anymore without getting some relief!" Terry said, "There is a pee can for you right under your cot."

The three men drifted off to sleep and enjoyed a refreshing night's sleep. At least, that is what Tom thought. Later in the day, Terry confided in Tom that he experienced some stressful moments during the night. It was pitch dark in the shelter. At some point, Terry was awakened by Ray feeling around for his pee can. Then Ray had to get up and stand over him, one foot on each side. This done, Terry realized the can was only inches above his head. In the inky darkness, he was thinking, "Don't miss the target!" Soon he could hear the urine dropping into the can. Dribble dribble, squirt squirt. Dribble dribble, squirt squirt. It seemed to go on forever! All the while he worried, "Don't drop it, don't miss it, and don't spray!" Finally

Terry Bostian's camp where Tom & Ray Sr. hunted a weekend. (Tom Massett photo)

Raymond L. Massett, happy to be at "Deer Camp!" (Tom Massett photo)

Ray finishes and carefully puts the loaded can back under his cot, only inches away from Terry's head. He could smell the warm, salty aroma of fresh urine. Damn!

Doubling Up on a Buck
By Tom Massett

For my family, our style of hunting is preferably tracking on snow in the Adirondack Mountains. It's not to say we only hunt at those times. That is when we have found it to be the most enjoyable and successful. My brother, Jim Massett, has a hunting camp located near Inlet, NY, and close to the entrance to the Moose River Recreational Area. We've hunted this location since we were old enough to carry a deer rifle. Our Pa before us first hunted here in 1932 and continued to hunt there until his final year of life in 1992. I always remembered Pa's words, "Tracking a buck is like turning the pages of a book."

In November 2002, Jim and I left his camp just about daybreak to drive back in the Moose River access to see if we could pick up the buck track Jim had seen driving out the night before. About 2 ½ miles in and on the Seventh Lake Mountain side of the road, we picked up his track. I took the track first while Jim planned on going down the road further and then heading up Seventh Lake Mtn to try and get ahead of the buck, or at least close the distance between the buck and us. As it turned out, the buck had circled up the mountain and then back down and crossed the road where now Jim picked up the track.

About 45 minutes of following the track, I came back to the road and saw where Jim had now started tracking. The deer went down through some green stuff, crossed a creek, and then headed up a mountain we call "Wildcat." I hurried along, hoping to catch Jim, as I knew he would be moseying along on the trail. When I caught up to him, we talked in hushed tones as to what we should do next. Jim said, "I'll give you twenty minutes to make a circle and see if we can get this deer between us." I said, "Okay," and swung down to the right, hit an old skid road, and then headed up the mountain in the direction the buck was traveling. After 15 minutes, I climbed the ridge that I expected the buck to be on. There I saw the buck track had already passed through. A short time later, Jim came along and we decided to continue as before, only this time, I dropped off the left side of the ridge and hit a small stream, which had good cover of evergreens on both sides. I turned to my right, following the creek upstream and parallel to the ridge on my right.

I had only gone about 200 yards and saw the track coming down the ridge and joining another deer, which I guessed was a doe. They both were moving upstream in the same direction I had been traveling. Soon they were joined by another deer track. I looked the tracks over closely and guessed the third track was a smaller buck interested in the hot doe. They zigzagged back and forth across the creek several times and then the deer I guess to be a smaller buck climbed the ridge to my right, where Jim was moving to. The snow conditions were getting a bit noisy by now because it began to thaw. I stood listening for a few minutes and heard a noise behind me. Turning around, I saw Jim following me and the deer. I gave him a short whistle and motioned one deer had headed up the ridge. Jim swung back and up the ridge, while I continued following the other two deer.

And so on we traveled. The tracks started to look fresher with clear imprints in the snow. Now it was harder to be quiet and each step in packing snow made several sounds. A deer's hooves are pointed and much smaller than a man's foot. They noiselessly slide into the snow while the back hooves step right into the track the front hooves made. The wind was blowing slightly and right at me. One to three steps at a time, then look and listen. Suddenly, I heard a noise to my right and down off the ridge came a deer running. I raised my gun and got the crosshairs on him. It was a spike horn with about 8 inch spikes. Jim had jumped the deer, seen his back side, but not his head.

The buck hit the tracks in front of me and began running along them. After a short way, he also walked along, following the same tracks. Jim soon came into view and I had signaled to him that it was a buck, but a small one. Jim turned back up the ridge and we continued on. Around 15 minutes later, I heard a sound of a deer running ahead of me and slightly to my right. I waited a few minutes and then eased over. The bigger buck and doe had climbed the ridge and by the tracks, it appeared the smaller buck followed. It looked like the smaller one had ran back down the same tracks and turned back up the creek. "Could this mean the bigger buck had chased him away?" I thought. I decided to sneak up to where the running deer had come from. As I said, the snow was now packing and soft, so I would slide my feet into the now, much like in cross country skiing as to make as little noise as possible. As my head peered over the top, I heard deer run out but very close. One went left, while the other directly away. I only caught a flash of tail. The deer in front of me was only 25 yards away, but hidden by a small spruce tree. He turned around and lifted his head looking for his lady friend. Big mistake! I could tell he was soon to bolt and I knew I would have to shoot fast. Even so, experience has taught me to raise the gun slowly whenever you have a standing deer. They will surely catch a movement if you pull the gun up too fast and run before you ever get it to your shoulder. So, I slowly raised the gun and fired one shot from my Remington 30-06 Model 742, hitting him in the neck and dropping the buck. He was a nice 9-point buck.

Jim showed up a short time later, took my picture and asked me if I needed help. It was almost all downhill from there, so I could make it on my own. I followed the top to the ridge, backtracking Jim to where I could turn down to

Tom Massett and the 9-point buck he took on Wild Cat Mountain. 2002

the skid road I had followed earlier that day. About 2 ½ hours later, I had the buck in the back of the truck and headed back to camp.

To me, it is always good to thank God for a successful hunt, which I did. This one was very pleasing to me as Jim and I did it together. Thank you Lord for family, hunting buddies, the Adirondack Mountains, and the elusive whitetail deer.

Ice Cave Mountain Hunt
By Tom Massett

The 60s & 70s were the absolute best decades for hunting the Adirondacks. The Massetts were always looking over maps and trying to figure out where the best hunting and the biggest bucks could be found. They put in an awful lot of physical work in getting to some of these places. The following story by Tom Massett will give you an idea of how strong their "Spirit for Adventure" was!

In 1969 we had two tents out of which we hunted. The first was on Ice Cave Mountain, about 4 miles in from the parking area at Indian River and the second one was reached by crossing over Ice Cave to the head waters of the Natural Hatchery Brook at the base of Canachagala Mt. That tent was a little over 8 miles from the parking area. We put that one there due to the fact that it was one of the last places logged by Gould Paper Co. and in the previous year my friend, Dick Jones and Jim's brother-in-law, Charlie Bartlet both killed big bucks near there. Dick shot a 16-pointer (ten natural points on one side and six on the other) while Charlie bagged a fine ten pointer. Brother Jim shot a big 8-point and I took a decent 9-pointer.

We used the first tent for a base camp while we spent most of the time hunting out of the Natural Hatchery Brook tent. To leave home on a Friday night, right after work and then drive up to Limekiln plus the 20 mile drive back to Indian River and then load our gear onto our homemade deer carts, cross the river, up the trail, then over Ice Cave Mt. on the summit trail down to the crossing at Natural Hatchery and turn left following a skid road a quarter mile to the tent took a bit of effort. We often would be stumbling along at that point laughing and a bit silly. It would be 1 AM or after before we completed the trip. Then up around 5 AM for breakfast and out the tent flap before first light. Looking back, I wonder how we did it. Anyway, we always planned on taking off the third week of the season which usually was the best week to find the bucks in full rut. Most of us were construction workers and did not have paid vacations. Brother Ray and I were steamfitters out of Local #818, while Jim was a sheetmetal worker out of Local #58 both located in Syracuse NY.

One morning during the third week, I left the tent to head south and then east crossing over the lower end of Ice Cave, then south again towards North Lake.

There wasn't any snow on the ground and the leaves were covered with frost. I came to a small creek which had a log about six inches in diameter lying across it. The water was around a foot deep and I could have crossed it easily or with a run and jump cleared the creek. Instead I decided to walk across the log. Big mistake! I had my 280 cal.

With the Remington Model 742 in the crotch of my left arm and began easing across the log. Suddenly, without any warning both feet slipped out from under me and I came down hard on my back across the log. The barrel of the gun struck a rock in the water while I held on to it tightly. It knocked the wind out of me and I struggled to keep from falling in the creek. I finally got up and struggled to the bank. I checked over my body by wiggling it around and found no broken bones. Then I raised the gun to my shoulder to sight down the scope. What the heck! I couldn't see anything through the scope. I lowered the gun to look it over and then noticed the stock, just above the pistol grip was broken and the bolt that holds the stock in place was bent so that the end of the stock was about 4 inches higher than it should be. Hence, I could not sight down the scope.

I unloaded the gun, held on by the barrel and attempted to swing the butt end of the gun, baseball bat like, against a tree in the hope I could bend the bolt back into place. It didn't work. So back to the tent I went. The rest if the day was spent taking the stock off, pounding the bolt back into nearly straight, reassembling the parts, tying the cracked stock with rope and then resighting in the gun.

The following morning found me back in the same location. I was a bit surprised to come to the exact same spot as the day before. I looked down at the log and said you're not going to get me this time and then crossed the foot deep water with my 18 inch high Lacrosse boots. After crossing I eased along, one or two steps and then listen. Again it was frosty with noisy, frozen leaves. In those days my hearing was very good and often would hear deer moving before seeing them. Around 15 minutes after the creek I could hear deer running. Up a hundred yards and to the left three deer ran into a group of spruce trees. The last looked like a nice buck. They went out of sight before I could get them in my sights. I waited. A couple minutes later out came a doe running and not far behind a big buck! She ran broadside from my left to the right and right through a nice opening. I raised the gun and put it on the opening. The buck ran right up to the opening and stopped just short of it behind a big hardwood. I could see his nose and his rear end. I held on the opening waiting for him to make his move. Come on you S.O.B. I said to myself. He didn't move. I waited and waited for what seemed like 5 minutes. My gun began to waver until finally I had to let in down. That's when he bolted across the opening. I started shooting; boom, boom, boom and then boom. The last shot I thought for sure I hit him as he ran across the small skid road I was standing on. I eased over and began to check his track for hair or blood. Nothing! The last shot had hit right into the center of the only log across the skid road I was standing on. I felt sick to think I had missed him. I started tracking them on the leaves which is quite easy on running deer. They circled back into a draw to the area they had first came from. Then they started walking. Around a half hour later and about two hundred yards from where I shot, I followed two tracks. One swung left and down across a small swamp while the other walked parallel to it. I followed the one going straight and soon came out to a gravel road. I could then see the track was not fresh and so I retraced my steps back to the track which crossed the swamp. When coming up out of the swamp the track turned right and a short way from there a fresh scrap was made under an evergreen bough. I knew they were close, but where were they? One step and listen as my Pa had taught me. When I got to the scrape, I looked down to see that big bucks track in it. I looked all around. I could not see them. One more step and then I heard a deer bound out in front of me. Blowing as it went. It was too thick to see it. I only went a short way and stopped. It continued blowing. There was no wind and by now the leaves had softened up. I felt like trying to sneak over in that direction, but I knew I shouldn't. I suspected by the sound of the blowing that it was a doe. She blew more than twenty times. Finally, right to my left, I heard a deeper blow not 30 yards away. Soon, from behind a tree a nose and rack appeared and then the neck of a big buck. I eased the safe off and slowly raised the gun. One shot put him down. A nice 10-point. I'm sure it was the same buck I had missed two hours earlier.

  The next day, brother Jim, Dick Jones and I went over and made a pack out of him and carried the buck to the skid road near Horn Lake where we would later put him into our deer cart for the trip out to the truck. Five days later he weighed in at 190 lbs even. It was a great week of hunting!

Rememberin' a Hunt at North Lake
(A Father and Son Adventure)
By Terry Bostian

Background:
  Sharing time in the hunting camps throughout the Adirondacks and learning lessons from stories told at the end of each day's hunt during dinner around the campfire have become valuable and cherished adventures over the past 35 or so years. While our hunting was often limited to weekends, many memories and lasting relationships were developed deep in the wilds of the Adirondacks. The adventure that follows is a sample of one of the many memorable hunts along the way that helped form our wonderful bond with the Massetts and Harts and others over the years that continues to this day. The memories will last forever in our minds and the Bostian's heartfelt thanks to them for including us in their family traditions.

The Hunt:

With 3 inches of snow on the ground and more predicted to come during this particular mid-November weekend in the early 1990s, we made plans midweek to head to North Lake to hunt some whitetail bucks. At this time in our life, my wife and I were living and working near Oswego, NY and Brian was working in Rochester, NY. For this particular weekend, with the weather prediction indicating good hunting conditions up north, we met in Oswego after work on Friday and headed to North Lake with gear and boat in tow. After we excitedly arrived at North Lake at about 9 PM that evening, and after launching the boat, we headed toward the north end of the lake since the roads around the lake were still closed to the public. We followed the haunting and beautiful images and reflections of the tree lines along each side of the narrow lake as we traveled northwards with the motor quietly pushing us along. We would take a right turn and follow up into the Black River to a point where we could go no further due to shallow water. There, securing the boat at the shore, we unloaded the boat and commenced our travel on foot to the tent located near Hardscrabble Lake, a mile or so in the distance to the east.

About 45 minutes after leaving the boat, we arrived at the tent with packs on, which were filled with provisions to replenish what we would consume during the weekend. This was to ensure that others who would venture in after us would have plenty to eat. Upon unloading our packs and building a fire in the wood stove, we recounted our blessings with anticipation of tomorrow's hunt as we prepared to hit the bunks. Excitement was brewing!

We had already been discussing during our hike in where we would like to start our hunt in the morning and decided we'd head toward Ice Cave Mountain. One of us would hunt the west side toward Canachagala Mountain and the other would hunt the east side along the north branch of Black River heading toward Horn Lake.

After breakfast the next morning and in anticipation of things to come, we headed back down the same trail we had come in on the night before and headed towards our planned destinations. As we were rounding the north end of the lake, we came across a single deer crossing the trail we were on. The deer tracks were heading along a small stream coming down from the north. We never thought much more about the tracks as the day was young and we had many more miles to cover in hopes of locating a set of big, wide-staggering tracks of a mature whitetail buck. So we continued toward our planned destinations.

After about another 30 minutes of walking before we would head our separate ways, we voiced our concern that we had only seen one set of tracks since we had left the tent in a little over an hour. As Brian headed east, I decided to cut into the stream drainage area that we have been paralleling since leaving the lake, just to see if the deer may still be heading in his original north direction. Sure enough, about 200 yards off the trail we had been on, the deer tracks were present and were still heading north. I backed out of the area and retreated to the main trail and continued toward the Black River.

After another 20 minutes or so, I decided to cut into the drainage to see if the deer was still heading in its original heading. Within about 200 yards, the tracks confirmed it was still heading north up the center of the drainage. I followed the tracks for a distance to see what the deer was up to. After a few minutes, I came across a small sapling where the tree bark was peeled from the trunk and laying on top of the snow, indicating it was a buck with antlers. Now the pursuit was on. It was time to get more serious about this deer because he may be a keeper. Again, I backed out of the area to the main trial and headed north again to circle the area in hopes of getting ahead of him and spotting him before he saw me.

Progressing on the main trail that was known to cross the Black River up ahead, I came to a spot where the buck had crossed over the trail and was entering the lower ridges of Ice Cave Mountain towards the Horn Lake area. After cautiously following the tracks for about 400 yards, I spotted a doe meandering through the saplings. About 50 yards from her, I spotted movement which turned out to be a buck. I thought, "Boy, this is like what you read in books, but I only wished Brian could be here now to share in this moment."

As the deer was not spooked, I took my time in leveling the 308 Savage bolt-action onto the deer chest cavity about 125 yards away. With the scope crosshairs on the center of the deer, "BOOM" the shot rang out. But to my dismay, there was no reaction from the deer. What happened? Did I miss? I remember thinking, "No way!," but I must have. After racking in another round, and as the excitement mounted, I leveled the gun and held steady again, this time leaning and clinching onto a nearby sapling for stability. Again, "BOOM," but this time the deer lunged forward and bounded about three or four steps as he crashed to the ground and out of sight. I thought Brian had likely heard the shots and may be on his way over if he was not involved with a deer at the time. It was just a short period of time before he came upon my tracks and located me. We exchanged a few words before heading to the deer. By this time, we figured the deer would have had enough time to have been dead. This would ensure the deer would not get up, if wounded, and run away – thus enabling us both to experience the hunt together.

After reaching the area, we realized the deer had been hit, blood was there, but he had managed to escape. Now, the pursuit was really on. One of us stayed on the track while the other had a few minutes head start in circling off to the side in hopes of seeing him. As we approached the river, Brian had reached the river about 70 yards to my right, and I noticed him leveling his 44 lever-action Marlin rifle ahead of him. I looked, but didn't see anything in his area. Then all of a sudden… BOOM, and the rifle lowered. I figured he must have gotten him. I ran to the area where Brian had shot. Brian told me that the deer was standing in the middle of the river about 80 yards from him when he fired. The deer bounded and went out of sight. The deer was not giving up easily. We both wondered if our guns' sights were off and not shooting where we had been aiming. We continued on.

After crossing the river and following the tracks, we were studying an area of small beech saplings and evergreens. As we observed the area, we noticed movement off to the right where the top of one particular sapling, located about 30 yards away, was occasionally moving. None of the other saplings were moving. There was no wind at this time, so we wondered what was causing the movement. Sure enough, after a few moments and as we approached the sapling, the deer bolted from his hiding. BOOM, BOOM – two more shots were fired and the chase was on. After about 200 yards, the buck bounded from the brush, other shots were fired, as we continued our pursuit.

To make a long story shorter, we continued to follow the deer tracks as they returned to and crossed the river again, going downstream and about 50 yards exiting to the east side. Daylight was fading and we really started doubting whether we would be able to catch up with him before nightfall. About an hour after dark, we marked the spot we last saw him and planned to return the next morning. It took us about two hours to return to the tent that evening.

After we got a bite to eat, we gave some thought as to how this deer managed to escape our attempts to get him. Was it bad aim on several occasions or were our sights off? Possibly. After dinner, we marked two paper dinner plates with an "X" in the center with soot from the stove and placed the plates about 50 yards in a safe direction with a flashlight illuminating the plates. Two shots later confirmed that our guns were still sighted properly. We were ready to return to the deer in the morning, yet still confused about how this deer continued to elude us.

After breakfast, we returned to the site of the deer's last seen spot. Brian took the track while I proceeded ahead circling to another vantage point higher on the ridge. With Brian in pursuit on the track, after 20 minutes or so, I heard another BOOM that caused me to reverse my direction and head to where the shot was fired. As I approached the area the shot came from, I was pleased to see Brian preparing to field dress a fine eight-pointer. After a hug and congratulation or two, we captured this moment both of us to cherish for a lifetime. The rest of our trip was joyous as we recounted the events.

Typically, we would butcher the deer ourselves, but this particular time we took the deer to a deer processor. We stood and watched as the cape and hide were removed. We counted the bullet holes and counted seven. Six of the bullets apparently managed to miss vital areas that would have killed the deer. However, with the last bullet, Brian was able to put the deer out of its misery.

L to R: Brian Bostian with his father Terry on an earlier father-son hunt. (Bostian family photo)

After pursuing and tracking a deer for several thousand yards while crossing and re-crossing a river and after firing several shots, a memory of a lifetime was created.

Gim'me Them Peas!
By Terry Bostian

One of my initial hunting experiences with the Massetts and Harts occurred in the late 1970s. At this particular time, their tent was in the Santanoni Preserve area, northeast of Long Lake, near Newcomb, NY. After returning to the tent one evening during dinner when stories were shared of the events of the day, the plates were being removed from the table. Just a couple of us were finishing our meal when Ray Massett Sr. announced, "Who wants the last of these peas?" One by one, the responses came, "Not I," "Nope, not me either."

I didn't realize that no one wasted food in camp and all leftovers were saved for the next meal. In the past, they had routinely experimented with creating ways to use all leftovers the best they could. Fruits in the morning pancakes, I could understand, such as bananas, blueberries, or the such.

Massett said, "Come on now, somebody's got to finish these peas." There was a period of dead silence followed by, "Well, I guess we'll just save them for tomorrow morning's pancakes." Immediately with that being heard, I blurted out, "You what? Put peas in pancakes?" The others chimed in, "Oh, yea, if they don't get eaten tonight, he'll put them in our cakes in the morning."

"Gim'me them peas," I blurted out. I couldn't envision looking down at pancakes in the morning with green peas looking back at me. I figured that if I was going to have to eat them, I'd rather eat them at the end of our spaghetti meal than breakfast.

Since that moment, we've shared many laughs about the peas over the years and, as you can imagine, it's usually shared at breakfast time with the group.

All Culverts, Washed Out!
(A Hunting Adventure with Tom Massett)
By Terry Bostian

It was the second weekend of the 1995 deer season. Friday night started out routinely with me finding my way back to our tent setup in the Moose River Plains. When I finally arrived at the parking area and left my vehicle, it was around midnight, due to me getting a late start that evening. I noted that Tom's pickup was parked in its usual place where he typically parked.

I remember just crossing the river with only a mile-and-a-half to go before reaching the tent. We always left an aluminum boat near the crossing for our trips back and forth across the river. A rope tied to the front of the boat provided access to the boat from either shore. I was about halfway to the tent from the river crossing when it started raining around 2:30 AM. Arriving at the tent, Tom had a gentle fire going making stepping inside a welcome experience. It continued to rain throughout the night.

In the morning it was still raining, but harder. After a hearty breakfast and with raingear on, we each headed in our separate directions in search of a buck. Being early in the season with several weekends to go, we'd be covering as much ground as possible in hopes of finding some good deer sign. This would allow us to develop a good understanding of where the deer would be located and prepare us for upcoming weekend hunts.

After traveling in the rain all day, it was during late afternoon I heard a tremendous roar in the direction of the river some quarter mile away. Curious, I proceeded to the river's edge to view what would be in store for us on our way out tomorrow. What I found was that the river water was overflowing the riverbank on each side. The water level had raised about five or six times its normal level, from 2 feet to about 10 or 12 feet.

After hunting until noon on Sunday, we headed from the tent towards the parking lot. Arriving at the river, we walked in knee-deep water for about 60 feet before getting to the boat, crossed the river, secured the boat to a tree on the far shore and continued on our way to the parking lot. Upon reaching the top of the last hill before the parking lot, and about a quarter mile away, we heard a float plane taking off from the nearby lake. Both of us, not saying a word, were in amazement, because we had never before ever heard a plane in this area and thought the lake too small for planes.

Upon arriving at our vehicles, we each had a business card from the local DEC officer (Gary Lee) placed under the wiper blade on our vehicles. On the back side of the card, something like the following was written:

"Hi guys, all the culverts between here and the main road are washed out. Drive to the river ahead, leave your vehicle, walk to the lake ahead, and we'll be back to pick you up at 5 PM."

Following those directions, we were picked up at 5 PM and flown to Seventh Lake. We could not have flown from the smaller lake due to the weight of two extra people. The flight afforded us tremendous views of the swollen rivers below. Getting a ride back to Syracuse later that evening, we wondered how long it would be before we could return for our vehicles. Turns out, it took about three weeks for the roads to be temporarily repaired. A month later we were able to drive in and get our vehicles

We still have the DEC officer's business card as a memoir from that weekend of hunting.

Ken Hart

Ken Hart was 10 years old when the great wind storm of November 25, 1950 struck NY State. The wind gusts were over 100 mph and everyone was talking about it. His older brothers and uncles were up in the Adirondacks during the storm, fortunately they all returned safe and sound. Brothers Dickie, Don, and Brud weathered out the storm. Dickie told him all about the storm and how it laid all the trees on the south side of Mitchell Ponds Mountain flat. This is when Kenny started to take an interest in their camps and adventures. He began taking trips to camp not long after this.

Ken was the youngest of 11 children in the Hart family. He was born on October 28, 1940. Just before his 14th birthday, his brother Don let him use his gun for a while. Two weeks later in mid-November, the woods were still dry, so they were doing drives. Ken was out with them and Don wanted Ken to carry a rifle, but brother Dick said, "No way, he is still too young!" Don argued with him and Dickie gave in. Ken was allowed to carry a Model 8 Remington in .32 caliber.

Ken was the last of the watchers to be posted. When the drive started, a big deer was moved. Ken could hear the drivers barking and making noise. That big deer had walked to within 20 yards of Ken before he realized it was there. When he looked behind him, he could see this big racker looking at him, Ken turned and fired twice at the fleeing buck. The buck was hit and bleeding. When everyone showed up, he told his story.

Dick followed the tracks while Don and Ken made a swing in the hardwoods on the ridge. Dick caught up with the buck down by the creek and put him down for keeps. It was a beautiful 10-pointer and Ken's first buck!

On October 28, 1956, Ken was thinking about making the long walk out to church, since it was Sunday morning. His brother Dickie told him, "It's your birthday, just go out to hunt and enjoy yourself!" Ken left camp with his rifle and headed over towards his favorite spot near Kings Clearing. There was a new road put in the year before that ran near the Red River. He walked down that and then walked a skid trail that angled over towards the base of Wildcat Mountain. There was a big rock that lay along the side of this skid trail. Ken sat down on that rock to watch for a while. He had watched the hillside above and below him for about 45 minutes, when here comes 2 doe bounding along below him. The weather was warm and dry. He could easily hear the does running off and out of sight. Then he heard another deer behind him. This deer came running out of the spruces and into the skid road only 20 feet away. One look showed him it was a real nice buck. Ken quickly brought his .300 Savage into play and dropped him right in the road. He counted 10 beautiful points on the rack. It was truly a happy 16th birthday and it was only 10:30 in the morning!

Ken hunted quite a lot with his brother Don. On one hunt they were using their friend Lloyd Weigel's camp. The camp was set up near Natural Hatchery Brook. When they arrived at Lloyd's camp, it had been raining hard and steady. The brook was way over its banks and the tent floor was flooded. They got a fire started, moved in, and dried out the tent while the water went down. The rain had passed on so the men went out hunting. Ken went down near the brook and then slowly hunted his way out towards the road. Don was farther over near Canachagala Brook. When Ken got out on the road, it was late in the day. He knew Don would be coming along soon and the thought crossed his mind that he might push something out to him. He stood in some cover just off the road edge and watched.

Ken wasn't watching long when down off a little knoll and out into the road walks this 8-point buck. Unknowingly, Don had started this buck and the deer was circling around behind Don. The buck was only 25 yards off and looking right at Ken, who had his rifle cradled over his arm. Ken thought if he moved in slow motion the buck might stand until he shot. It did, and the buck fell dead in the

Ken Hart with 8-pt taken in deep snow on Moose River Ridge, Saturday after Thanksgiving 1989. (Ken Hart photo)

middle of the road. Don heard the shot, but wasn't sure where it came from. Ken stayed off the road and in the spruces. When Don made the road, all he could see was this dead buck, and nobody around, until Ken stepped out. He was pretty happy. They had a buck hanging the first day, despite their wet start!

The Migration Trail

In 1989, Don Hart and Ken had been hunting out of Don's camp near Long Lake. They had celebrated Thanksgiving there, but it was snowing every day and Don had his belly full of walking through the snow. He was calling it quits for the deer season. After that, Ken went down to Limekiln to hunt in the Plains. By then, there was a lot of snow on the ground. Ken had his great nephew Roy with him. With the deep snow, Ken decided to hunt the Moose River Ridge where the deer migrate into the plains to yard.

Roy and Ken hunted their way onto the ridge and they could see that the deer were really moving. By 1:30, they had seen a couple of small bucks and about 20 doe. As they approached the end of the ridge, they separated and took a watch. Two others in the party were hunting below and ahead of them. Ken saw a buck run into some spruces below him so he just watched. Pretty soon, the buck came out

Don Hart's 8-pt buck with a 23 ¼" spread. Moose River Plains (Ken Hart photo)

and Kenny nailed him. It ran down the run, bleeding heavily, and dropped 50 yards off. It was a nice 8-pointer.

That evening Ken called Don up and told him to come on up, the deer are moving in! Don, at first, argued that he was all done, and No, No, No! But he finally gave in and went up.

This trip in they hunted along the Moose River. Ken and Roy were kind of pushing for Don who was on a trail that ran parallel to them. Ken and Roy jumped several deer. The boys didn't know it, but one of them was a real nice buck. It ran over toward Don and they heard him shoot twice. They found him with an 8-point buck with a rack that spread over 23 inches or about as wide as his smile!

The Biologist

C.W. Severinghaus (Bill) graduated from Cornell University in 1939. He devoted his life's work to understanding the world of whitetail deer. Many of his studies were conducted in our Adirondack Mountains. Bill, along with researcher Jack Tanck, developed a system for aging deer that the average layman could use. He did extensive work in the Moose River Plains. This included a study of trails and runways deer use in getting to their wintering yards. There was a deer trail index guide developed to determine the foraging ability of yarding deer. Deer were trapped and tagged. Some of these deer were recovered almost 20 miles from the trap site. He also proposed the first doe seasons to reduce severe over-browsing of winter deer yards.

A doe season in the Adirondacks was not welcomed by most Adirondack deer hunters. They were used to seeing lots of deer around and wanted to keep it that way. Bill wanted to protect the winter deer yards and the quality of the deer herd. In an effort to reduce the number of deer using the Plains winter yards, the state sold hundreds of antlerless deer permits for $1.00 each in the early 60s. Many hunters didn't like this either, but the permits always sold out.

The Moose River Massacre

Severinghaus knew he had a tough sell with the hunters so he held a number of public forums to educate the public. It was during the last week of February in 1964 where he got into big trouble with the public. In the Moose River yards, Bill and some conservation aides killed 54 deer. Bucks, does, and yearlings were taken. This was to determine the health of these deer in an over-crowded yard with deep snow. They took reproductive organs and leg samples, and left. This occurred during a generation of sportsmen who's parents had lived through the "Great

Depression." They were taught not to waste anything, and this was looked upon as a senseless waste of life. News of this, along with photos of desiccated deer carcasses, made 76 newspapers statewide, and, from Chicago to Bangor. Headlines read "Unwarranted Slaughter" and branded it "The Moose River Massacre!" Sportsmen were madder than hell. Bill received threats of bodily harm and death too!

In time, things settled down, the deer survived and Bill continued his studies. There were no more headlines! Even now, when I talk with some people who remember this (Ramie Massett and Don Hart), they are still bitter. I personally hope Bill's studies warranted the slaughter. Severinghaus was a pioneer in whitetail study. Many of his works are still used to date. Bill died in 2007 at the age of 90. He was well respected despite this incident.

In Retrospect

The 1950s, 60s, and 70s were wonderful years for deer hunting in the Moose River Plains. There was lots of deer around and the Massetts and Harts knew the area well. There were up to 18 members in their group. This included a few close friends, but mostly family (cousins and grandchildren). They were not all into camp at one time, and many were not trackers, but they sure knew now to hunt. They

November 1985
Three of the best deer trackers in the Adirondacks. L to R: Raymond L. Massett with his sons, Tom and Jim. His close nephew "Brud" was also a topnotch tracker.

had some outstanding years to remember, like in 1947. In 1966, the season take was 3 bears and 19 bucks. In '67, they took 23 bucks. Back in 1957 with a full camp of hunters, they brought in 7 bucks on Saturday and 4 more on Sunday. Mahlon Stone told them, "You will never realize what you have here until you lose it!" Those wonderful, abundant years started tapering off around 1970. By 1975, they were down to 5 bucks out of the camp.

Raymond L. Massett, the patriarch that started it all, enjoyed the camps right up to his final year. The DEC laughed when the 81 year old hunter applied for a remote camping permit. He told Terry Bostian that when he was in camp, he felt just like a 16 year old kid! Ray passed into the arms of our Lord a year later in 1992. His legacy lives on!

Raymond Massett enjoying a cup of java at their Indian River camp. (Tom Massett photo)

Dick Hart with his 140 5/8 11-point taken in 1969. (Don Hart photo)

Joe Spurchies brought home a buck & a doe.

Setting up camp near Ice Cave Mountain. (Tom Massett photo)

In some areas the far side of the Moose River was better hunting! (Tom Massett photo)

The early season crew at the Balsam Lake camp. (Ken Hart photo)

Bringing one out! L to R: Ken Hart, Brian Bostian & Bobby Hart.

Two big 10-pointers and a crotch horn from the Adirondacks. (Tom Massett photo)

Results of a late season hunt. L to R: Roy Hart, Jim Hart, Don Hart & Ken Hart. (Ken Hart photo)

Dennis Gipe

Dennis was raised in the Liverpool area of Syracuse, NY. His father, Dennis Sr. and an uncle, Cliff, introduced him to hunting at an early age. It was a very rocky start. At 14 years of age, he was on his first bow hunt with his Uncle Cliff and older cousin Cliff Jr. They were hunting near Tully, NY and had split up to watch from their own stands. The agreement was, if anyone hit a deer they were to return to their vehicle and blow the horn. Everyone would then participate in tracking and bringing the deer out.

It was very windy that day. Dennis hit a buck, returned and blew the horn, but no one could hear it due to the wind. He began tracking his buck alone. He soon caught up with 2 men tracking the blood trail his buck was leaving. These guys tried to tell him that he had no business being in the woods and to go home. They also told him it was their deer they had wounded. The deer was found dead shortly afterwards and it was Dennis' arrow sticking in it. About then his uncle showed up and things got straightened out. A tough beginning for a 14 year old.

Unfortunately bad experiences didn't stop there. At age 16 on opening day of gun season, Cliff Jr. shot a buck and a doe. Both Dennis and Cliff were dressed in blaze orange and had their guns unloaded while dragging the deer out. On one of their rest stops, they heard a shot ring out with some leaves and dirt flying into the air by Dennis' leg. Dennis thought it was his cousin and yelled, "I told you to unload your gun!" But it wasn't his cousin. Up the hill from them was an older guy sitting up against a tree. They confronted him and he admitted shooting. He thought the deer was crawling and never saw the 2 boys dressed in blaze orange. Can you believe it? These instances were giving Dennis a very insecure feeling about hunting Central New York public land. He wasn't going to wait for number 3 to happen.

Like many of us, Dennis learned his basic skills of hunting in Central NY. His grandfather, father, uncle, and cousin all contributed too. He attended his first deer hunting seminar at the Great North East Sports Show. It was given by Jim Massett and during the presentation Larry Benoit was introduced and spoke to the group. Jim was always his hero and role model, but listening to two deer hunting legends was the perfect experience. He attended all of Jim's seminars that he could. Stories of hunting the deep woods intrigued him, so in 1996, he headed north to the Adirondacks.

He stayed at the North Star Inn at Eagle Bay to begin with. His wife, Kristen didn't come from a hunting family. It was hard for her to understand why all these weekend trips to the mountains were necessary. When he started driving back into the Moose River Plains, the mountains and unbroken woods were intimidating. He was afraid of getting turned around and lost. Dennis started out by trying short trips into the woods and coming out. He began to build confidence and learned how to navigate through the woods. In 1999, Dennis took his first Adirondack buck by tracking.

He was 3 hours on the track before he had a shot and dropped it. It wasn't a huge buck, but he had successfully tracked it down for the kill. He was elated and thought, "Wow! This works!" His next thought was, "Now just where am I?" It took him 3 seasons to venture into totally unfamiliar country. He had his map and compass and now a buck. Everything would work out OK.

Another good thing happened to him around that same time frame. Dennis knew about where Jim Massett's camp was at Limekiln Lake, but always lacked the courage to stop in for a visit. Finally in 1998, he stopped to say, "Hello." Jim gave him a warm welcome, just like they were lifelong friends.

When he learned Dennis was staying at the North Star on weekends, Jim invited him in to use his camp. Dennis didn't want to overextend his welcome, so he declined Jim's offer. Two years later, Dennis was high up on Little Moose Mountain in the plains, when he heard the steady crunch, crunch, crunch of approaching footsteps. Dennis was tracking a buck and had stopped briefly to eat his lunch so he went on full alert. The crunching materialized into Jim Massett.

Dennis with his first Adirondack buck. 1999

A Little Moose Mountain buck taken by Dennis. (Gipe Photo)

When Jim recognized Dennis, he gave him a big, friendly bear hug, and then they enjoyed a good lunch time visit on the mountain. By the time they parted company, Jim insisted no more North Star! Dennis was to come and stay at his camp. Dennis agreed and was extremely happy about it. Bunking in with a bunch of veteran deer trackers was an added benefit. He could always pick up valuable information in conversations after each hunt. Listening to those veterans talk, he sometimes wished he was born 2 or 3 generations earlier, just to experience what they did.

It was while talking with his friends at Jim's camp, that he realized how important it was to know where you were at all times in remote areas. The death of Art Birchmeyer, one of their good friends, served as further proof. Dennis invested in a good GPS and was very grateful that he did. Now there was no guessing. He knew exactly where he was at all times and knew the most direct route out. His confidence in going to far away places on the Topo map soared.

In 2000, he took his second Adirondack buck. It was up on Little Moose Mountain and the track alone got his adrenaline flowing. It was a big track with lots of drag. He saw where the buck rubbed a tree and was amazed at how far away his front hooves were from the rub. The tracks eventually led him to a hot doe and 2 smaller bucks. He went crashing right through the top of a windfall to drive them away from the doe. He could smell his rank tarsal glands saturating the air before he even saw him. He also followed it though 2 trees spaced 16 inches apart. This caused him to think that maybe his rack was not so big. When Dennis finally caught up with the buck and killed it, the rack had a 20 ½ inch spread. Bucks will tilt their heads and do whatever they have to when going through narrow spaces. In 2001, he hunted with Joe Esposito and Lynn Murphy in an area just north of Big Moose Lake. He took his 3rd Adirondack buck there.

Got Cart?

In 2002, Dennis was again way back in and coming off Little Moose Mountain. He stopped briefly when he thought he heard a woman's voice. In fact, he did hear a woman's voice. There were 4 people – a mother, father, son and daughter. They had hiked in for a 3 day hunt and the father and son each killed a buck within a ½ hour of each other. They were on the trail bringing them out. Dennis could see they were struggling to move the deer. He told them he had a deer cart out on his car and would come back with it to help them. The father looked like he had his doubts and was quite surprised to see Dennis return with the cart. They were from Massachusetts and were very grateful for the New Yorker's hospitality.

What Difference Does it Make?

In 2003, Dennis was staying at Jim's camp at Limekiln Lake. In the morning Jim said, "Why don't you and I head out together and see if we can get a buck?" Dennis quickly agreed thinking, "I'm going out on a hunt with a legend and my personal deer hunting hero. How good can this be?!" The 2 men drove off into the plains together. Just before the Moose River, they located a nice buck track in the road. Jim said, "Listen, I want you to take this track and hunt it down. Before you start, run me about a mile or so down the road and drop me off. You can pick me up in the same place around dark." Dennis brought him down and saw him enter the woods.

When he returned to start tracking, he could not locate that track. Here was an opportunity to prove himself to his mentor and he couldn't even locate a track crossing a road. He spent an embarrassing hour looking for it and nothing! At 8:30 AM, he ran up to the Otter Brook Trail and parked at the gate. Soon afterwards, he found another track heading up towards Kittle Cobble. He jumped this buck out at 11 AM and by 1:30 PM he caught up to him again. He jumped him out of his bed and couldn't get a shot at him before he made it to some dense spruce trees. Dennis thought, "The wind is at my back. That buck is going to turn back into it once in the cover." He ran as fast as he could up the hill to watch for the buck leaving the evergreens into the wind. It worked perfectly and he dropped the buck right there. He took several photos, dressed out the buck, and started pulling it towards his car.

What difference does it make? A buck is a buck! (Gipe photo)

He couldn't make it all the way out with the deer and still pick up Jim at dark, so at last light, he ran down the trail to his car. Another member at camp had picked up Jim and waited for Dennis along the road. Dennis said, "I got a buck!" Jim said, "I knew you were going to get that buck!" Later at camp, Dennis told Jim the whole story and Jim thought it was pretty funny. A buck is a buck!

Trail Camera Addiction

In 2008, Dennis tracked a buck right up to a big sign post tree. This tree was way up on Little Moose Mountain and was almost 2 feet in diameter. The tree appeared to have been rubbed for decades! He decided right then and there that he would set a trail camera covering the activity at this tree. He didn't own one at this time, but by early next fall there was one at the tree. The sign post tree really lived up to its name. Deer, bear, bobcat, coyote, fisher, and anything with a nose visited that tree. This tree fell to the ground over the winter. Dennis was amazed to see that this tree was still being visited and even rubbed when down!

He then started investing in trail cameras. Before he knew it, he had 6 trail cams set miles apart, all over the central Adirondacks.

On one occasion, he set a trail cam in mid-July. Because of all the summer foliage, he could not mark its location with his GPS. In the fall after the leaves had

The sign post tree visited by a buck on a rainy night. (Dennis Gipe photo)

fallen, he returned for the trail cam. Those woods sure looked different! After 40 hours of searching, discouraged and about to give up, he said this prayer, "Lord, help me find my trail cam. I don't care if I fill my tag or not this season. I just want my trail cam!" As Dennis was leaving that area for the last time, he noticed a rock that seemed familiar. He looked to his left and there was his trail cam! The trail cam recorded a fair amount of activity, but no great pictures. Also, he didn't get a buck that fall. He noticed that trail cams were taking up to much of his hunting time and were altering the direction of many hunts. His trail cam activity was scaled way back!

Around 2005, Dennis decided to try some of the new Kifaru ultra-light camping systems. He had a teepee style tent and a foldable compact wood stove that together weighed about 13 pounds. He could have heat, cook, and dry his clothes inside this tent. The stove would generate good heat for about 1 hour before dying off. This outfit along with some food and a sleeping bag could put him almost anywhere in the mountains for a weekend hunt. He just loves this outfit and is very comfortable with it.

Endurance

On October 29, 2006, Dennis was listening to the channel 9 forecast for the central Adirondacks. They were predicting 6 to 8 inches of new snow over the week-

Wind fallen sign post tree. (Dennis Gipe photo)

Buck visiting the sign post tree even after it had fallen. (Dennis Gipe photo)

His ultra light Kifaru tent and stove in good weather. (Gipe photo)

end. "Perfect," he thought, "I'm going to grab my Kifaru outfit and hike into Brook Trout Lake and have 2 days to work a buck on new snow." He told Kristen he wasn't going to be hunting with anybody. He told her where he was going to be and that he would be home Monday morning. She understood the whole plan, so Dennis left for the trailhead to Brook Trout Lake.

The weather leading up to his weekend was rainy. The ground was saturated and all the streams were swollen. Driving into the plains towards the trailhead, Dennis crossed the Moose River. It was then he noticed how high the water was. It still didn't dawn on him what his trail conditions were going to be like on the hike in. All he was thinking of was tracking, snow, and deer hunting. When he got to the trailhead, there was a trapper coming out with hip boots. He said to Dennis, "You're going in?" Dennis replied, "Yes." The trapper then said, "Boy, there's an awful lot of water!" To which Dennis replied, "I know, I know." However, he really didn't know.

He had weighed his pack at 65 pounds with enough provisions for 3 days. It was also 5.4 miles in to the lake. The first half is mostly uphill. An hour of walking in, he came to his first creek crossing. The 2 step rock top crossing is now knee deep. He doesn't know why he packed them, but he had some ultra-light waders in his pack. He made the crossing dry. His second and last creek crossing was a bigger stream that came down from Twin Lakes. This was waist deep, fast water and caused him to reconsider his destination. He was 1 ½ hours in and it was getting close to dark. Dennis was stubborn and took off his pack. He carried it across. He stumbled a couple of times, but kept his pack dry.

It was only a short distance now to his campsite. He was in there in September, planning ahead for this hunt. He had cleared out an area for his tent and cut and covered a supply of dry firewood. As he approached his site, he could see that it was flooded. The cover was gone from his woodpile also. Everything was soaked! Things were not looking so good.

In the dark, Dennis found a place to erect his tent. Then he had to forage for wood dry enough to start and hold a fire. That was a big challenge. He remembers blowing on the smoldering wood so close that he singed both his eyebrows. He did manage to get a weak fire going, but the exertion of the day and coming in left him exhausted. The heat from the stove brought on sleep. He remembers the rain changing over to wet snow around 11:30 PM that evening.

When he awoke in the morning, the fabric of the tent wall was pressed tight against his face. He pushed it away and then looked outside. There was a generous foot of snow on the ground now. He couldn't believe how quickly it fell. Now he had to make a decision. He could hunker down for a couple of days and hope things improved or he could make his way back out to the vehicle. There was no hunting with a foot of wet packy snow. The spruces were all loaded and the hardwood whips were all bent over. He dreaded the trip out, but that's what he chose.

It was still snowing big, wet, heavy flakes. Everything was wet going into his pack and he had used nothing, so it weighed closer to 80 pounds. The first creek crossing going out was now over his waist. He hung onto alders and bent over trees to make his way across. The snow was getting deeper. Then when about halfway out, he slipped on a rock under the snow and hyperextended his knee for a split second. This scared him when he realized what an injury would mean in this situation. He cached his pack and continued on with only his GPS and fire starting equipment. He finally reached his S-10 Blazer tired and dehydrated. He had not had anything to drink since the day before. This was beginning to affect him mentally.

The Blazer was buried under snow. He found it hard to believe this was the parking area he had left the day before. He heard a chainsaw running in the distance. Then a Bronco and another vehicle drove up through the snow. There were 2 young fellows in the Bronco. Dennis asked them "Are you guys heading out?" They were. He said, "Well, I'll follow you out if you don't mind. You guys have been cutting? Did you just come to a tree down?" They replied, "We've been cutting since 8 this morning." Dennis asked, "From where?" They said, "Oh, about a half mile back." It was only 10 AM now and Dennis couldn't believe it. There were trees across the road everywhere, some of them quite large. Dennis had a chainsaw in his trunk so off they went. They hooked up with other people trying to get out. This included about 9 farmers from Batavia, good strong bodies. They didn't make it to the Limekiln gate until 2 AM. It wasn't any picnic out on the plowed state highways. The power was out, cars and trucks stuck all over, and National Grid trucks were working on the lines all over the place. He drove as far as Old Forge, then stopped at the Adirondack Lodge. He walked into the lobby and told the guy at the desk, "Listen, have you got anything at all. I'm so exhausted, I'm about to pass out." He looked at Dennis and said, "I've got one room, but it isn't clean yet." Dennis replied, "I'll take it just the way it is." The clerk said, "We've been going crazy the last day or so. The troopers just left here, looking for some guy that was in remote country." Dennis said, "Really? What was his name?" The clerk replied, "I can't remember. It was kind of an odd, short name." Dennis asked, "Was it Gipe?" "Yea, that's it," the clerk answered. His wife became very concerned and called the authorities. Dennis called Kristen right away to let her know he was safe and would be home in the morning. Actually he caught only a few hours of sleep and headed home. The weather bureau recorded the snowfall officially at 17 inches, but Dennis thought it was definitely higher in some areas. Three and a half days later, he walked in to retrieve his backpack on less than 2 inches of snow!

Joe DiNitto

Joe DiNitto was raised on the family farm in Marcy, NY. He had a natural inclination to hunt. The farm, surrounded by some of the best hunting in the state, was a great place to start learning the basics. Joe's father, Tony Sr., was a dedicated deer hunter. He never discouraged Joe or his older brother, Tony Jr., from hunting or shooting sports. One season when the boys were still relatively young, Tony Sr. went hunting in an area near Bridgewater. Back on the farm and between chores, Tony Jr., pushed a spike horn buck out to Joe and he promptly killed it. They couldn't wait to tell their Dad all about it later when he came home with nothing. This began a great family tradition of deer hunting.

Joe's first Adirondack hunts were on the Gull Lake and Twin Sister Clubs. They were located on the west side of Route 28, just south of Thendara. Tony Sr.

Joe DiNitto's first buck taken on the family farm. (DiNitto family photo)

3 nice bucks taken by the DiNitto family. L to R: Tony Jr., Tony Sr. & Joe.

and his 2 sons would do small pushes to each other days, and then maybe take up a watch until dark. It was always enjoyable hunting with his father and brother, but now that Joe was getting older, he had a "wanderlust" feeling gnawing at him. He wanted to see and hunt other areas in the Adirondacks. Larry Benoit's book, "*How to Bag the Biggest Buck of Your Life*," fueled his desire to see different country even more. Tracking bucks was a fascinating hunting technique, that would also satisfy his craving to see more country.

First Tracked Buck

Joe was hunting an area near South Lake one fall. He was twenty-two years old and very comfortable in hunting the big woods. There was almost 8 inches of snow cover now, so reading deer activity signs in the snow was easy. On his way back to the lake, he cut a big track heading west that wasn't there in the morning when he started out hunting. It was close to 4 PM, but Joe started tracking that deer. It was late in the season also, and Joe noticed that this deer started to feed. This is when he saw the buck leaving some decent antler tracks in the snow. A short while later, he saw the buck get up out of his bed, take 2 bounds and stop. Joe dropped him cleanly with his 30-06 pump. This short successful hunt gave Joe a tremendous amount of satisfaction. He had found a promising track, followed it, reading sign, and positively identified it as a buck he would shoot. Then he tracked it to his bed and took it for his own. He was hooked on tracking!

The coming seasons saw Joe doing nothing but tracking. He worked out an agreement on the farm where, if there was tracking snow in the Adirondacks, he would be hunting until he got his buck. Tracking became his passion, gaining knowledge with every track he followed. He insisted on hunting alone so he could be totally independent. He did not want to be out at the truck by dark or meet someone up on a ridge for lunch. Joe just wanted to concentrate on the buck he was tracking. With this mindset, he would hang up big mature Adirondack bucks regularly. Joe's father often told him, "Don't ever let anyone tell you that you can't do something. Always go with the attitude that you can do it." This is how he feels about every track he decides to follow.

An Outstanding Record

Joe is in his late 40s now and still a long way from slowing down. Looking back over the past 20 seasons, he has taken 18 mature Adirondack bucks that averaged 6 ½ years in age. During this time, he has only hunted 3 to 5 days of each season. Some were only one day seasons! I have looked over Joe's trophy collection and it is mighty impressive. He went right to school (by himself in the woods) on tracking Adirondack whitetails after his first success. I would say he is holding a Master's Degree right now!

This is How It's Done

I have never heard a clearer or simpler analogy of the tracking process than what Joe DiNitto offers. If you are interested in tracking and you don't "get this" without asking a lot more questions, you best give it up!

Joe will hunt anytime there is snow on the ground. However, the post-rut and the early part of the season, before the pre-rut begins, are the easiest times to track a buck down. Of course, you can successfully track them during the pre-rut and rut, but bucks regularly travel long distances during that period, so it is hard to get close to them. They are out looking for does and they don't eat much. Joe states, "You don't lose 20% of your body weight by stopping for lunch!"

When Joe enters the woods to hunt, he is only looking for a big buck track. He has his rifle slung over his shoulder and is walking along at a good pace. He is only interested in finding a big track. Joe likes to see a big print, with a long stride and a wide stance. This indicates a big chest on a heavy buck. The track may also appear to stagger. Other signs will fill in the blanks – urinations, rubs, antler tracks, etc.

This is what you look for, a big print, long stride, wide stance with a little stagger to it.

Anyone can follow deer tracks. It's knowing when to go fast, when to slow down, and when to move ultra-slow. In the post-rut, a buck is in the process of slowing down and regaining the weight he lost during the rut. He likens the buck to a man coming home from work. If the deer is moving right along, then it's on the four lane highway heading home. For no apparent reason, the track will then hook left or right. This is getting off the thruway. Then it will start meandering, "He's in his neighborhood and close to home." Once he gets home, he will go right to the refrigerator and grab a snack, meaning eat fern roots, tree mushrooms, or maybe beechnuts. Then he will go to the bathroom and hit the couch or bed. You want to slow down when he gets off the freeway and more in his neighborhood. When he grabs a snack, go ultra-slow, you are very close. Joe recommends doing a lot of looking, then moving one foot slowly before shifting weight and looking again. One of you will see the other first; make sure you see the buck before he sees you. It isn't easy!

On Saturday, October 23rd, 2005, Joe was looking at TV when a travel weather advisory for Warren and Hamilton Counties appeared on the screen. He went to his computer and one of the blogs said there was 4 inches of snow on the ground. He had no knowledge that any snow had fallen in the state until then. He gathered his hunting gear together and had everything ready by midnight. The next morning he drove up to Inlet and there was no snow anywhere. He picked up a new Topo map anyway and headed up to Blue Mountain Lake. When he drove through Blue Mountain Lake village, the state was plowing the highway. By then it was 8 AM. He pulled over into a parking area and started looking over his new Topo map, thinking, "Where am I going today?"

The east end of Blue Ridge ended just short of Cascade Pond. Joe decided to look over near the pond and if he didn't find a good track, he would go right up on Blue Ridge. He accessed the area through the Lake Durant campground. Two hours later, he was climbing Blue Ridge. High on the ridge, he jumped out some does and fawns, but there was no big track to be found yet. He continued on and was approaching a saddle when he found what appeared to be a big deer track. There was snow in the tracks from melting and dropping snow. It was hard to find a clear print, but the stagger was there, indicating a big deer. Joe tracked it for about 25 minutes. During this time, he saw where it had rubbed and twisted a one inch sapling. A few minutes later, he rubbed one of the biggest trees he had ever seen a rub on. Shortly afterwards, the tracks turned sharply to the left and uphill. Joe thought, "Alright, we are off the highway and into his neighborhood." A little further and the buck stopped to feed. "He is in his house now, time to go real slow. Let him make the mistake, not me." Joe imagined himself to be a moving tree stand now. One slow deliberate step at a time with lots of looking. Larry Benoit would call it his "Death Creep." Joe didn't go very far and there was a very fresh buck track. He knew it had to be the same buck.

Now the air temperature had warmed up and snow was dropping and saplings were springing back up. All this movement was beneficial for Joe. After moving about 20 yards in 40 minutes, he saw the buck raise its head to scratch an area on his back with an antler. The buck was about 14 yards off. When the buck brought his head down, Joe couldn't see him. What to do? Grunt, wait or move? His hand moved towards his grunt tube then stopped. He took a slow step to the right, nothing. Then back and slow step to the left. He could see it's back. Boom! He died only a short distance from his bed. The buck was a 9 ½ year old 10-pointer and dressed out at 191 pounds. This was at 12:30 on the second day of the season, in an area he had never hunted before. Joe called his brother Tony to help bring out the buck. He met up with him just after 4 PM. Joe was soaking wet from all the wet snow falling off the trees, but he tagged out on a beautiful ADK buck and enjoyed a memorable hunt.

Did this hunt sound easy? It was nowhere near as easy as it appeared to be. However, this is the type of hunt Joe has perfected. He didn't waste any time hoping to see a buck in the woods, but instead hunted for the track of a buck. He didn't slow down until he got into that buck's neighborhood. This next part is where 90% of deer trackers screw up. You have to discipline yourself to move ultra-slow and close with your buck. Before Joe saw that buck at only 14 yards, he was wet, cold, and starting to shiver regularly. Most hunters would have stepped up the pace and at best would have seen a quick flash of brown as the deer bolted. Even under the best of circumstances, the buck often escapes. Joe states, "With snow on the ground, 80% of the time I will be within 100 yards of a mature buck before the end of the day. If you get this close to a mature buck, then his first rule of the hunt comes into play: "Always put yourself in a position to get lucky!"

A Tough Year to Hunt

In 2007, there was almost no snow to hunt on. Joe had been out on 2 days earlier in the season with a thin snow cover, but didn't produce a buck. Now he was down to the last 5 days of the season. Joe confided in a friend, Steve that he was starting to get nervous. Not about killing a deer, but not getting the snow needed to do it on. This was on a Tuesday and they were forecasting a chance of snow. On Wednesday, they got a dusting of snow. Overnight brought 2 or 3 inches and Joe thought, "That's enough, I've got to go!"

Thursday morning saw him driving deep into the Moose River Plains. He found an old buck track crossing the road. It most likely crossed last night during the snow squalls. Joe started tracking it, one of only 3 he has ever taken from a road. The old track led him through an old feeding and bedding area. The buck re-crossed the road and this time, the tracks looked considerably fresher. Joe had been

Taken on Blue Ridge above Cascade Pond by Joe DiNitto. The results of a perfect stalk.

Taken on the last snow of the season.

on his tracks about 3 hours when he saw where the buck began feeding again. He thought, "Now this time, that buck should be here!" Joe started his slow, stealthy approach on the buck's track. It led him up to the top of a small rise. After gaining the top, he had only taken 2 small slow steps when he saw the buck looking right back up at him. Joe could see his head, neck, and the bases of his antlers. That was all. He put the crosshairs right below his head and shot. The buck made one leap and stopped. Joe swung onto this shoulder and shot again. The buck mule kicked and took off, but not far. Joe was soon looking down at a 7 ½ year old 8-pointer. He was very happy with this buck, because there was actually very little chance for any snow to finish off the season with.

1997 was another stressful year for Joe. He never carried his rifle in on a hunt until November 27th. Joe loves to hunt, so having to wait that long for snow was pretty tough on him. On that same day, he shot a 5 ½ year old 8-pointer on Canachagala Mountain.

Joe DiNitto with his 20 inch 9-pointer from the snow laden woods. (DiNitto photo)

The Snow Laden Woods

One season, Joe and his son, Joe Jr. went up for a hunt together. They were using Browning micro medallions in 7mm 08 caliber. Before entering the woods, it was discovered they only had one clip between the 2 identical rifles. Joe let his son have the clip and he would hunt his as a single shot. On this day, there was 8 to 10 inches of snow on the ground. A recent snowfall had also loaded the trees, making visibility poor in the woods. Many hunters do not like this condition. However, the snow was soft and quiet and the snow camo clothing made the hunter difficult for the deer to spot.

Joe was on a snow-filled track by mid-morning. He never saw the track clearly, but the width and stagger gave it away. Joe busted out the buck prematurely. However, he didn't wind Joe, so he waited 40 minutes to let the buck settle back down to normal. When back on the track, Joe saw where the buck had raced off 4 or 5 hundred yards and then watched his back track. Satisfied that he wasn't being pursued, he traveled on and began feeding. When Joe saw this, he went into his "stand hunting routine"; take a step, then stand and wait. He moved about 50 yards in this manor, hoping the buck would make a mistake. He slow-stepped around one snow-covered limb and he could see the buck looking back at him through a hole

Kindred spirits of the hunt. L to R: Jim Massett, Joe DiNitto & Steve Grabowski. (DiNitto photo)

in the snow-covered limbs. Joe brought his rifle up and shot. The buck never moved! He lowered the rifle and ejected the shell casing. A new cartridge was slipped in and Joe looked for the buck. He didn't expect to see it, but damned if it wasn't still there! This time at the shot, it mule-kicked and ran off. Talk about luck! The buck was down and dead 75 yards from where it was hit. It was a 20 inch 9-pointer that dressed at 176 pounds.

The only other advice Joe would offer is to shoot your deer rifle reasonably often, two or three times at a target once a year is never enough. Get comfortable with your rifle and confident. When your chance at a big one comes, you will be ready.

Bob Kratzenberg

Bob Kratzenberg was born in Utica, NY, but raised in the town of Forestport. How and why he became an avid hunter God only knows. There was no family history of hunting at all in his background. His father gave him his first gun when he was still a youngster. It was a single-shot shotgun. Bob remembers his father's words after receiving his gun, "You won't use it as much as you think you will." Boy was he ever wrong! Bob was out with it every day looking for partridges, rabbits, and later deer. Hunting was in his blood in a big way. His first deer rifle was a Winchester Model 94 Big Bore in .375 caliber. Eventually, he bought a Remington Model 6 pump in 30-06 caliber and this is what he still carries now.

Bob killed his first buck with the Model 94. Like most first bucks, it wasn't a great rack. Four points in all with a spike on one side and 3 on the other. The next few years saw him hunting with a group or a buddy. He participated in deer drives, still hunted and sat on runs. After sorting all this out, he knew that deer tracking was the most enjoyable and effective hunt for him. He would still go out with a buddy or a small group, but when they hit the woods, Bob was off on his own. A handheld radio would keep the hunters in touch when necessary.

Bob likes to hunt the area between McKeever and Thendara and east of Route 28. The middle and south branches of the Moose River border many of the hills and ridges there. Gaining access to this country often involves a canoe ride across the Moose in various locations.

Team Work

Tony Charzan, Keith Kanclerz, and Bob were in along the Moose one morning doing some pushes. Tony had an 8-point down before 8 AM. They dressed out the buck and left it. Bob suggested they hunt towards Tooker Mountain. Over on the mountain, Tony called Bob on the radio and asked his whereabouts. Bob told him he was on the south side of Tooker. Tony told him to come around to the north side. He was on a track heading up that way. Bob headed around to the north side at a fast clip, just in time to see the buck and shoot at it. Another nice 8-point down. By the time they had both bucks down to the canoe, it was dark.

Hunting along the Moose River, Keith Kanclerz, Tony Charzau & Bob. (Kratzenberg photo)

Bad Timing

During the 1987 season, Bob hunted out of Duane Merrick's camp off the Wilson Pond Trail. During the hunt, he got up onto Blue Ridge and saw the cave camp that Vileni Merrick used at one time. The cave was interesting, but didn't appeal to him for a stay. He thought it might get wet inside at times. He hunted around one alder bed that a big buck had all rubbed up. After 3 days hunting it, he gave up and went home.

The next day, Dennis Ruth called him up and wanted to know if he wanted to do a hunt up at Duane's camp. Bob said, "No, I just came back from there!" Dennis replied, "Why didn't you call me? I would have gone up." Bob said, "Well, I just wanted to be a loner on this trip." Long story short, Dennis went up to camp that afternoon. The next morning, he shot that alder bed buck. It was a beautiful 10-pointer!

The Alder Bed Buck shot by Dennis Ruth from West Branch, at Blue Mt. Lake, Wilson Pond Trail. (Kratzenberg photo)

Dennis Ruth camp on Wilson Pond Trail. L to R: Bob & Tom Kratzenberg. (Kratzenberg photo)

Grindstone Creek

In the fall of 1995, Bob, Tony Charzan, Wayne Kwasniewski, Rick Ritter, and Steve Shutz set up a tent camp back in along Grindstone Creek. On opening weekend, they were all in at the campsite. The forecast that day was for rain. They were not worried about the weather since they had a warm, comfortable tent with a big fly covering the whole outfit. They planned to spread out and hunt their way over to a huge rock near the Adirondack League Club line between 4th and 3rd Bisby Lakes. They agreed to meet around 11:30 AM.

It started raining not long after leaving the tent and by mid-morning it was coming down steady. Bob was at the big boulder by 11 and it was coming down in

Grindstone Creek Tent, 1995. (Kratzenberg photo)

buckets! He was soaked right through to the skin and decided nobody would meet here today. In the morning on the way up, he had crossed a beaver meadow and the water was only ½ way up his LaCrosse boots. Now the water was up to his balls! Grindstone Creek drains most of its water from Golden Stair Mountain. It was a running torrent now! Arriving at camp, he could see that everyone was back and inside.

Their square box john located out behind the tent had water right up to the seat. There was water over the floor of the tent and the stove made it feel like a sauna. Everyone was up on their cots and nursing a bottle of Burgermeister beer. They said, "What do you think?" Bob replied, "Let's make ourselves at home until the water goes down!" The water rose a good 3 feet during that storm. When the rain ended, it seemed to go down just as fast.

The Lock and Dam Camp

For a couple of seasons, Bob had a tent camp set up below the lock and dam on the middle branch of the Moose River. The river was navigable for a small boat and motor for about ½ mile of river below the dam. The area around Nick's Lake was easily accessible from their camp. Bob's brother, Tom, planned on hunting out of the camp that season. Tom had been working for his brother recently. With the season coming on strong, Bob bought him a new Model 94 .32 Winchester Special. Then when season opened, they moved into the tent camp on Friday evening.

The next morning they hunted a hill Bob called Haystack Mountain. Bob told Tom to go over to an old skid road where a number of new rubs and scrapes showed up. Bob would hunt around the back side of the hill and then down Tom's side, but further over. They would meet up later on near a small stream. Bob heard a deer go off the hill top, but he didn't see it and no shots were heard. Later when they were to meet up, Bob saw his brother walking his way looking very pissed off. Bob said, "How did you do?" Tom replied, "I can't believe this happened! I was standing there on watch, when just like you said, this buck comes running down from the top. It wasn't just any buck, he was HUGE. He had a real wide spread and points sticking out all over the place. He stopped 50 yards off and I had a clear shot. When I pulled back the hammer and shot, it just went click!" Bob said, "Why didn't you pull the hammer back and try it again? It may have had some grease, ice, or whatever slowing down the hammer." Tom replied, "I didn't really know what to do with that monster standing there. Finally, I jacked another shell into the chamber. The action noise got him running, I shot again, but it wouldn't fire."

They decided to go back to the boat and take it up river to camp and get Tom a rifle that worked. On the way upriver to camp, Bob was running the motor with Tom in the front of the boat. Bob was looking ahead when he saw a big wide 8-point buck standing right on the river edge. This buck was also only a short dis-

Lock and dam camp just below Old Forge, middle branch Moose River. (Kratzenberg photo)

tance from their tent. Bob grabbed his rifle, and just about had the buck sighted, when Tom stands up. This of course rocks the boat and Bob's rifle. The buck now ran over near their tent. Bob said, "What do you think?" Tom replied, "Well, my gun isn't shooting. Let me get out and I'll follow him over and push him across to you." Tom followed the deer's tracks and caught him standing right by the tent. Tom double clicked on the buck with his rifle. Then it starts running off along the river and he clicked twice more and a third shot actually fired, but missed. The guys couldn't believe it. They had 3 easy chances at 2 big bucks and blew all three! They gave up this camp site because cold weather in the last half of the season ices up the river. It's a tough job getting the camp out.

Jones Mt., left, Nelson Lake & Little Round Top, right. (Kratzenberg photo)

A Challenging Hunt

Most of Bob's hunts were by himself. He started out one morning looking for a good track to follow along the south branch of the Moose. There is thicker green cover along that stretch, so it's a good place to look for a big track. He got up as far as Remsen Falls, then went north across Tooker Mountain. At 8:30 AM, he found a good buck track and began to follow. The buck was cruising and led him over near Jones Mountain. Instead of going up onto Jones Mountain, he stayed low in all the brushy stuff along Nelson Lake. Bob kept thinking he might get a look at him there but then he went cruising down the south side of the Moose River. He passed within sight of Bob's canoe and then headed up a ridge. Having hunted this area many times before, Bob remembered a rock outcropping that the bucks liked to bed on. The tracks did lead over to it and he had bedded there for a while, but left. Bob didn't realize how far he was behind that buck until then. Now the track was fresher and it was leading him right out into the point where the middle branch met the south branch. By now it was 3:30 PM. There was an alder bed and a big beaver swale on the point. Bob then thought, "I got him. I've got about 1 ½ hours before dark. I'll just take my time and do it right."

Bob carefully made his way out into the point going "slower than slow!"

Several minutes later he put out a doe and just caught a glimpse of the buck with her. No shot. The 2 deer bolted for the river on the point. It's a place where Bob has seen them cross many times. He raced out and around the alders to where he could see the river across the beaver meadow. Out came the doe and then the buck. The doe stopped in the wide open and the buck stopped behind the only alder clump in the meadow. Bob was all out of breath and shaking like a leaf in a breeze. He thought, "Come on, follow that doe!" The doe began to cross the river. The buck walked straight away then turned right toward the hardwoods. Bob had one shot as the buck entered the thick willow whips. The buck was over 220 paces away and when he shot, he was sure he heard a solid "smack" of the bullet hitting the buck. At the track, he found a little bit of hair, but not blood. When the buck got into the hardwoods, he found a small pool of blood. That raised his hopes. Instead of climbing, the buck cut down lower. There was another popular river crossing for deer just up the stream. He went out to the river and watched, but the buck didn't show. Almost dark and back on the track, he saw where the buck bedded and left. It was dark now, so he left for home and would return at first light.

When Bob returned the next morning, he quickly picked up the old track. From where he left the evening before, this buck would travel about 20 yards and then bed up. After passing several beds, he could hear the buck leaving the next one. He noticed it appeared to have a stiff hind leg, but mentally that buck was still very sharp. Bob made some swings on the deer, but then find it within the circle. By 10:30, he still hadn't seen it well enough to kill it. The buck never traveled very far before stopping. Bob decided the next time he got close he would try to run it down. This worked out good and he was able to get off 3 shots to put him down and out. The buck had a huge hole in his back bone. Bob was amazed the deer could even move with such a wound. It carried a beautiful 10-point rack and died between Tooker Mtn and Nelson Lake. It took 4 hours to drag that deer out to his truck!

Shot in the Moose River

On one late season hunt, Bob was coming down a sand ridge heading toward the river on a track. The buck had bedded farther up the ridge and when he saw Bob, he stood up and then went down into the alders. Bob saw him also and stood waiting to see if a shot was offered. He ran over to where he could get a better view, but all he could see were bits of motion as he moved away in cover along the river. Then the buck turned out toward the Moose. By now, the buck had to be 250 to 300 yards away. It broke out into the river on the run and Bob had a clear, but long shot at the running buck. When his shot rang out, there was a big disturbance in the water by the buck. Bob thought, "By God, I might have hit him!" He ran down to the river as quick as he could, just in case the buck was floating down-

Robert J. Elinskas   119

1 ½ day tracking job, Bob Kratzenberg. (Kratzenberg photo)

It pays to be familiar with your hunting area. Bob has tracked plenty of bucks to one common bed on a rock outcropping. One day the tracks were leading to this bedding site. He approached from a different angle & shot this buck in its bed. (Kratzenberg photo)

Bob with a buck he killed in the Moose River. (Kratzenberg photo)

stream. He looked across and all over, but couldn't see the buck. Finally he spotted a snow-covered rock out in mid-stream that looked like it had blood on it (Bob is color-blind, but he has learned what the color of blood appears to him). His canoe was just about 1 ½ miles downstream. He was just thinking about going for it when he heard some gurgling sounds from behind him. He turned to see the buck dying in the water behind him. That buck had saved him a lot of work by tipping off his location!

Grunting

Bob uses a grunt call quite a lot, especially when the snow is crunchy. He has had bucks come running right up to him. He was hunting in the Big Moose area a couple of years ago when he found the tracks of a big buck with a doe. He had just started tracking them when, in the distance, he could see them run over the ridge he was on. He hurried on up to the top. He started grunting on the call and here comes the doe right up close. She took one quick look at Bob and off she went. The buck wasn't far behind her and he booked out too. It was a real big buck with at least 10 points or more. Bob shot twice at it and hit it at least once. He tracked that buck all day long until full dark. Bob guessed he hit it under the spine and over the lungs where it wouldn't do any lethal damage. It was tough to lose a buck like that one. He was outstanding!

Other Predators

One day, Bob was in the area of Nelson Lake when he came onto a fresh killed spike horn buck. Something had been eating on its hind quarters. He looked the carcass over, but couldn't find any bullet holes. Then some movement in a nearby windfall grabbed his attention and a huge bobcat went running out of it. Bob was thinking coyote at first, and then he saw the short tail. He shot it when it crossed a small opening. It later weighted in at 40 pounds. No more deer burgers for that cat!

40 lb bobcat that killed a spike horn buck. (Kratzenberg photo)

L to R: Tony Charzan with Bob Kratzenberg and the buck he waited 2 hours to finish off. (Photo by Keith Kanclerz)

The Long Wait for Help

Bob has taken some real nice bucks from Nick's Lake all the way down to McKeever. He shot a beautiful 21 inch, 9-point up behind the lake one fall. He was on his track for 3 hours and had bumped him a couple of times. Finally he caught him coming down the back side of a hardwood hilltop. He shot 8 times at him running through the whips and managed to hit him twice. That was enough to put him down, but he was not dead. Bob could see him lying in the woods below him and now he was out of ammunition. He called Keith Kanclerz on the radio and asked him to come over and finish off this buck. Keith had never hunted this area before so Bob gave him some instructions on just where he was located. Even so, it took him 2 hours to hook up with his hunting partner. Bob pointed out the buck to Keith and told him to shoot it. Keith said, "No, it's your buck, you do it!" The buck was dispatched and Keith said, "I thought you always carried 9 cartridges with you?" Bob replied, "I do, but I shot them all at the buck." Keith then said, "I only counted 8 shots." Bob said, "No, I shot them all!" They argued back and forth. Bob finally looked through his pockets and lo and behold, another shell was found. He had waited on that hillside for 2 hours for a cartridge he didn't know he had.

I Can't See Blood

Being color blind had been a big handicap for Bob. He cannot follow a blood trail on leaves. On snow, he has learned what blood looks like to his eyes, but on the terra firma, he is dead in the water.

Bob wounded a huge buck back in on a distant ridge one fall. He was on his hands and knees trying to see if he could locate any blood. Finally, he called up Keith Kanclerz. Keith operates "Keith's Taxidermy" in Forestport on Route 28. He is one of Bob's "go to" guys. He said, "Listen, Keith, this buck is huge! You've got to come up and look. I shot him right in his bed. When he came up out of it, I didn't think I had to shoot him again. Now, I'm kicking myself."

Keith followed Bob back in to where the buck was bedded then showed him the tracks leading away. Keith said, "You can't see that blood?" Bob replied, "No." Keith then said, "I could see this blood trail from that distant ridge. My God, it is 4 feet wide!" Bob said, "Really! Do you think we can find him?" Keith replied, "Guaranteed! There is no way in hell this buck is getting away bleeding like this." Long story short, the buck quit bleeding shortly afterward and they could not find him.

Taken on last day of season, 2 December 2012, one of Bob's shortest and easiest hunts. Antlers scored 146 and post rut dressed weight 142 lbs. (Kratzenberg photo)

Easiest Buck Ever!

It was the season of 2012 and Bob wasn't feeling good at all. He was down with the flu and down to the last 2 days of the season. His earlier attempts at putting a buck down didn't produce. The season ended on December 2nd and now it was the 1st. He thought about going out somewhere, just anywhere and watching from his truck, but his body wouldn't let him. Another day at home and off to bed early.

December 2nd saw Bob up early. Amazingly, his fever had left him and his body aches were gone. In fact, he felt damn good. He had to make the most of his last day of deer season, but where to go? The Moose River country had always been good to him so he drove up to his favorite crossing. The river was still open and there was just enough snow to track with. Bob paddled across, pulled out the canoe and climbed to the top of a low, nearby ridge. On top was a nice fresh deer track. Bob looked around and off to his right in the pines, he could see a deer standing there. Couldn't tell if it was a buck, so he turned his scope up to 9 power. He still couldn't see antlers, until the deer turned and started to run. Even though he had his rifle on the deer, he only had time for one hasty shot. Bob was not too confident in walking down to check for blood. Can you imagine the smile on his face when he saw that buck down and dead only 50 yards further. The buck carried 11 points on a gorgeous rack that later scored 146. Bob said it was one of his easiest hunts ever!

Deer Hunting Lesson

When Bob's son Kyle was still quite young, they went out to sit in a nearby tree stand together during muzzle loader season. Kyle knew the basics of shooting and how to use sights on a gun. Sitting patiently in a tree stand with nothing happening can be tough on a youngster. Kids get bored quickly. Bob wanted to see how he would do.

After climbing the tree stand, Kyle sat on Bob's lap and they began to look around. They weren't watching 2 minutes when Kyle whispered, "Dad, there's one right there!" Bob looked and sure enough, there came this 4-point buck walking right over toward them. Now Bob is right-handed, but he shoots like a lefty, off his left shoulder. He brought the muzzleloader up to his son's left shoulder. Kyle could pop squirrels off the bird feeder with a .22, but this rifle was heavy. He kept pushing the rifle away and finally whispered, "Dad, my other shoulder!" Bob realized his mistake and shifted the butt plate over to his son's right shoulder. The buck was

Son Kyle with muzzleloader buck. (Kratzenberg photo)

Bob's wife Kim also hunts. She has several bucks to her credit. This is her buck. (Kratzenberg photo)

close then. Bob lowered the front of the gun down and Kyle lifted it to align the sights on the deer. Bob whispered in his ear, "Make sure the sights are on the deer." BOOM! Kyle said, "Wow, did you see all that smoke, Dad?" Bob replied, "The smoke! Didn't you see your deer run and fall on the ground?"

Terry Perkins

Terry was born and raised in Troy, NY. He married his high school sweetheart, Diane Darling, right after graduation. He began working for the state that summer, starting as a counselor at a conservation camp in the Catskills. Next he began working for Fish & Wildlife in Delmar. Eventually, he moved up to the Warrensburg offices in the early 1960s. While at Warrensburg, he had taken the Forest Rangers exam. In 1967, he was awarded the position as Ranger at Stillwater. Terry and Diane moved into the Ranger Station in 1967 and stayed for 31 years. Terry was offered several promotions and a chance to move out, but turned them all down. They both loved the area, so why move away and possibly have regrets? As the years passed, they bought property nearby. This included a camp on an island that they improved to serve as a year round residence. After retirement, they moved less than half a mile to their island home.

Terry became a trapper through no initiative of his own. While working in Delmar for Fish & Wildlife, their resident wildlife trapper, Bill Hammersmith, took a promotion. Bill used to handle nuisance wildlife complaints that the state would get involved with. This could be anything from bats in the attic to bears in the basement. Terry was the "fall guy" for replacing Bill. Talk about a greenhorn, he had no previous experience with trapping. Fortunately, Bill was around early on to give Terry some helpful guidance on getting started. The rest was an adventure in trial and error. Terry had also made an acquaintance with Johnny Thorpe. Johnny was a well-known and very successful trapper. He also gave Terry helpful advice. Terry became responsible for a 5 county area: Washington, Warren, Hamilton, Saratoga, and Fulton.

Terry's first endeavor to trap fur was up in Stony Creek with Bert Morehouse in 1964, 1965, and 1966. His first attempts at skinning a beaver were quite a challenge! Eventually, he became very skillful at it after removing many hundreds of beaver pelts. Terry also became well acquainted with many of the trappers in the Adirondacks. The winter fur sales were great get-togethers for trappers to compare notes and see how well they did. He told me, "I've never met a trapper I didn't like."

Terry trapped the Stillwater area the very first beaver season he was in residence. In those days, they stretched the beaver pelts round. Now they use the Canadian method of stretching oval. He never learned the art of clean skinning in the field. Terry would rough skin each beaver and then take the casters and oil sacs, which are worth money also. He would occasionally save the liver. Beaver livers are large and are very good eating. The meat is excellent also, especially that section between the body and the hard flat section of it's tail. Terry calls it part of the loin. That hard, flat, hairless section of the tail is not what you want for eating. I am sure that someone at some time has tried it, so if you are out for a real adventure in cooking, go to it! The amber colored teeth of beaver also make some unique and beautiful jewelry. I have seen some beautiful necklaces, earrings, bracelets, and various decorations, all made with beaver teeth.

Trappers Camp

Terry and Diane live right in the middle of some of the best trapping country in the state. When trapping, he considers his home, "base camp." There was one season, he guessed around 1982, when he trapped out of a remote tent site. In the fall before that season, he located a campsite at the head of the Bog River Flow. His tent site would be near the outlet of High Pond off the west end of Low's Lake. He cut himself a generous supply of dry firewood and left the site ready for his late winter arrival.

Terry returned in mid-February to begin trapping. He was able to drive in part way over John Knox's property. Payne and Levi were actively logging portions of his 4,000 acre tract. From there, he drove his snowmobile in to his campsite. He took the time to set up a comfortable camp. A 9x12 wall tent was erected, with a woodstove and an old carpet for the floor. A winter tent is a whole lot cleaner with a carpet on the floor, because it keeps the mud at bay. The frequently thawing and freezing temperatures inside the tent, plus snow tracked in, can generate a lot of mud.

Building a sizable trapline from scratch takes time. Locating and putting in sets, plus establishing a trail between them consumes a lot of daylight hours in February. This first line of traps slowly, but steadily began to take shape and produce. At the end of the first full week, a personal friend of his came in to keep him company. John Connelly was a professor at Corning Community College. John wasn't a trapper, but he enjoyed his time spent in the mountains. It was good to have some company on his ever expanding line. When John left at the end of a week, Terry sent out 25 beaver pelts with him to be stored back at his base camp on Stillwater.

A few days later, their son Steve brought Diane in to spend a week with him. By now, Terry had 2 lines established. One was about 10 miles long and the other was 22. Of course, you can't always drive up to a set with the snow machine. Many of the sets were of the park-and-start-snowshoeing type. Once a good snowshoe trail was beaten down, you could move right along on it. Most of the area ponds had active beaver colonies on them. Diane made the daily check with Terry and saw many of the remote ponds.

One day they found a weather balloon with it's recording box snagged in a tree. The balloon was about 2 foot in diameter and was still fully inflated. Diane decided she wanted to have it for an upcoming party and conversation piece. For the next 10 miles she hung onto the balloon tether as they made their way from set to set. When they arrived back at camp, the string slipped through her fingers and her balloon sailed above the trees tops, free at last!

The Mother Lode

Just west of Darning Needle Pond was Fishpole Pond. Terry could stand in one spot at Fishpole and count 5 huge active beaver lodges. Four were on the pond and one was on the inlet brook. These beaver were also feeding on lily pad roots. Their fur was rich black and they were all fat and in great condition. Terry knew he

Terry out on his line with another beaver to skin. (Perkins photo)

Looking north from the end of Lows Lake – Tamarack Pond, left, and High Pond, center. Cat Mountain and Cat Pond, center. (Bob Elinskas)

Bringing back another beaver. With longer days and sunshine, it's good to be out checking your traps! (Perkins photo)

had wandered into a little gold mine! He set several of his traps there and they rarely disappointed him on each check. He also had sets at Ash Pond and Darning Needle Pond. He caught more beaver at those 3 ponds in one week than in all 3 previous weeks together. Terry was a busy man!

Back at the tent, he had built a snow cave to keep his rough skinned pelts in. This worked out well for storage. He did have some very minor damage from mice, but not enough to complain about. He had also brought in a fleshing board. It worked good when the temperature was just above freezing, however he just stayed with the rough skinning. There were too many beaver coming into camp. The last half of the season also brought better weather and longer daylight.

At the end of beaver season, Terry pulled his traps and camp out. Once back home at Stillwater, he had 2 full weeks of fleshing and stretching beaver hides. Terry admitted that the guys that can clean skin a beaver and those that could efficiently use a fleshing board had a big advantage over him. He had a fur buyer come up to his house and buy all the beaver, plus several otter that were caught incidentally with traps set for beaver. This was the only time he camped out for trapping. Running a remote trapline was a great experience. It was very rewarding knowing you were capable of doing it successfully.

Terry contributed to the Otter Restoration Program back in the 1990s. At first the program offered $400 for each live otter. This monetary incentive didn't create the needed motivation for producing many otters. When the offer was doubled to $800, that's when Terry joined in. Terry caught a few live otters for the project, but Doug Riedman of Old Forge, Gary Lee of Inlet, and Frank Webb of New York Mills were major contributors.

Trapping the Stillwater Area

Terry's home was surrounded by some first class trapping country. He could trap right from his home and be very comfortable afterwards. In addition, he could begin to finish and stretch the green pelts evenings and have a hot shower when done. To the uninitiated, beaver trapping sounds very simple. You set big traps and catch big rodents. Not so simple! Usually it is very cold with lots of snow. The traps are heavy, stabilizers and bait sticks have to be cut, and often holes have to be chopped out in thick ice. The animals are heavy and wet when caught. Rough skinning may be required immediately. Then when you get home, the hides have to be fleshed and stretched. This might be on a good day. Sound like fun?

A Difficult Day on the Line

Trapline conditions can vary greatly when the weather begins to warm up. Terry recalled one day when the snow was very deep and a brief, but intense warming period arrived. He was slogging along through wet snow and sinking down 16 inches in many places. On this particular day, every trap seemed to have a beaver in it. Then it was stop, rough skin the critter, put the pelt in your pack and slog on. About halfway through the check, Terry saw where a huge bear had crossed and re-crossed his snowshoe tracks ahead of him. The tracks were fresh! Terry was thinking that the rain and melting snow had driven him out of his den. He was probably hungry, too. "And here I sit with a half dozen greasy, musky, beaver pelts in my pack and smelling like one myself," he thought. Plus, there were beaver carcasses lying all along the line. This was not a good situation. It made Terry very uncomfortable. He kept looking around for the bear as he checked his line. He then thought, "Under these conditions, I couldn't outrun a chipmunk!"

He came to one piece of flowed ground where he had a set out in the channel and right in the middle of the meadow. Now the entire meadow was flooded with a layer of greenish water on top of the snow. The trap was 100 yards out into the meadow. Terry is wearing 16" rubber packs and he knows damn well that water will fill them up. He doesn't want to check the rest of the line and face the long walk home with wet feet. Terry took his boots off and then tried something entirely new to him; he snowshoed out to the trap in bare feet! He said to himself, "this is not a good thing to do!" He couldn't get the harnesses down small enough to grab his feet well. He had to keep his toes curled to keep his feet in the harness. Also, he had to concentrate on every move he made, especially with the water and slush pulling on the shoe. It was grim determination that got him out to the set, and sure enough, there was another damn beaver in it! Normally, it would be a blessing, but that day, it was a curse. Then he had to remake the set and haul the beaver back to the woods with him. Terry's feet and legs were rosy red from the prolonged icy water bath they endured. At least his feet were clean and dry for the remaining check!

Skinning, fleshing and stretching beaver hides is a time consuming part of beaver trapping. (Perkins photo)

Terry with a number of Stillwater beaver stretched "round." (Perkins photo)

The Reservoir Highway

Terry likes to trap during February and March the best. The fall trapping is OK, but the fur isn't real primed up like it is later on. Also, he uses the reservoir to access many of his trapping sites. The ice on Stillwater is usually good through March. However, in April and even late March, the ice will start pulling away from shore. When this condition starts, it makes it very difficult to get off and back on the ice. His traps are usually pulled by the end of March just for this reason.

A Cure for Migraines

Terry's father, Robert, would often take vacation time just to run traps with him. Bob was a good trapper and an excellent hunter. In the fall, they would catch a few beaver and then use the meat for fisher sets. They both took advantage of the high fisher prices during the 1980s. Bob was sometimes plagued with migraine headaches. He claimed that skinning and fleshing beaver hides would eliminate his migraines. He thought it had something to do with smelling the musk. Bob never suffered migraine headaches while beaver trapping.

Terry with a 35 lb bobcat he trapped. (Perkins photo)

Deer Hunting Stillwater

Terry told me that the Stillwater area is a great place to hunt deer. There is an awful lot of country to hunt with very few posted signs. There are a lot fewer deer around than there used to be, but if you enjoy working a track, you will seldom hit a line of posters. Terry always enjoyed tracking a buck. The day was always interesting when you had a buck ahead of you. Most of the time, you would get to jump him and some of the time, you would get to kill him. That was Terry's preferred method of hunting.

The Kettle Hole Buck

Terry was out by the road doing some work near his storage barn when 2 fellows that he was acquainted with stopped to talk. These guys did a lot of road hunting. One of them was crippled up and had a permit to shoot from his vehicle.

They never got anything, but they were out looking anyway. They had been down near the dam and while looking up the lake, a deer was spotted out on the ice in one of the bays. The reservoir was still open water, but the bays had iced over. This deer was almost a half a mile away, but through their rifle scopes, they could see antlers. One guy thought he might try shooting at it, but didn't. When they saw Terry by the road, they shouted, "Hey, want to see a buck?" They then told him their story.

Terry went back with them and saw the deer. He looked through their scope and sure enough, it had a modest set of antlers with maybe a 14 inch basket. The buck was up in a long deep bay that ended in what locals call "the Kettle Hole." They asked, "How are you going to get it?" Terry replied, "I don't know, but I will go back and get my rifle." Terry got his Marlin chambered for .35 Remington, then drove his truck as far as possible across the dam, toward the buck. There was a hill, that they called "the Bald Spot," between the truck and "the Kettle Hole." The rock ledge on this hill offered a view of the bay and looked like a bald spot, hence the name.

Terry didn't want the deer to wind him as he hiked over to "the Kettle Hole." While heading down toward the ice, he jumped out 2 coyotes and almost shot at them. As Terry approached through the woods, he could make out the buck still standing out on the ice. The buck was looking in Terry's direction, but was still 200 yards away. He was still back in the woods trying to conceal himself as he moved closer to the shore ice. He expected the buck to bolt, but he didn't. When 50 feet from the ice, Terry shot and missed. The buck still didn't move. He dropped him with the second shot.

When he tested the ice, he saw it was barely thick enough to hold his weight. It was only 1 ½ to 2 inches at best. There was open water only 80 yards south of the buck. He found a dry, soft maple pole about 18 feet long and moved about 20 feet out toward the deer. The ice under him seemed to be making tiny fracture sounds. He immediately reassessed his situation and went back to his truck and home. Diane and their grandson, Robert, were at the house. He filled them in on what was going on. They returned with him to "the Kettle Hole." This time, he was armed with a life jacket, pike pole, snowshoes, and two ropes.

Once back on the ice, he had a rope tied around his waist. Robert held this rope and payed it out as he moved toward the buck. Terry had snowshoes on and carried the pike pole and a shorter rope. He took a circular route out to the deer with the ice creaking all the way. He also noticed where those 2 coyotes had been laying on the shore, watching the deer. Going out toward the buck, he saw where one coyote broke through the ice and returned to shore. Terry was sure he was going through the ice at some point! He moved as close as he dared to the buck and then threw a loop over one antler and snubbed it tight. He tied this rope to the one that had been around his waist then followed it back to shore.

Terry was relieved and amazed that he did not fall through that ice. Together the 2 men pulled the buck to shore. They could see where the coyotes had bitten it several times. The buck must have taken his chances of drowning rather than being eaten on land. Either way, his fate had been sealed. Terry just gave him a quicker way out. Terry also guessed that with all the adrenaline flowing from the coyotes and being trapped out on the ice, he was going to be one tough deer. Not so though. He turned out to be one of the best eating deer ever!

The Lost Buck

Terry, his son Steve, and Terry's father Bob were hunting south of Stillwater Mountain. This was International Paper property before it became leased and eventually sold to Lyme Timber Co. The men all separated at first light and went their own way. Around 8 AM, Terry heard a shot ring out, but nothing more. If any of their group connected, a signal shot would be fired. Terry continued to hunt, unaware that Bob had shot and wounded a buck. The snow was patchy and this buck bled little, so the track was eventually lost. Bob suspected he paunched it.

Around 3 PM, Terry is heading north and in the general direction of his truck. Now it is also snowing big, heavy, wet flakes. Visibility was poor. He walked down into a deep gully he had to cross. Then, just ahead of him, he caught a glimpse of a deer's back and one antler. It was lost to sight quickly so Terry brought out his deer call and gave 2 bleats. The buck swapped ends and came walking right back to him. It stopped only 100 feet off and Terry brought up his Model 94 for a shot. The heavy snow had loaded the open sights, but he shot anyway. Walking over to the tracks where the deer fled, he found blood. With a heavy snow falling, the chase was on!

Terry tracked him for 15 minutes or so when he saw a deer bedded ahead of him. It appeared to be a doe, so he kept moving on the track. When the doe fled, he saw that in fact it was actually his buck! Damn, it could have all ended right there! The tracks now led him across a logging road and then the road to Big Moose. He was on the reservoir side now, which wasn't far away. Twice the buck had walked out onto a point and then turned back to the woods. Terry had enough of this, so he cut across to the far side of the next point and waited for the deer. The deer didn't show. Terry was hunting along the edge back onto this point when he spotted the buck. It had left the point and was now walking into the water. It was 100 yards out and up to its belly when Terry finished it off.

Now he has a dead buck in the water and it is getting near dark. It is also 32 degrees and snowing. Terry thought, "Let's just get this over with!" He strips off all his clothes. All of them! He covered them with his jacket and starts walking out toward the buck. What a sight to behold had a boat come down the impoundment! The water was icy cold and his tender feet were being tortured by sticks, roots, and rocks that were bedded in a layer of black, squishy muck. This made progress extra slow. He finally got out to the damn buck, who he now suspected of having this all planned out beforehand! Once the carcass was back on shore, he quickly put all his clothes back on. It was almost dark now. He left the deer there without dressing it out and made his way up to the road. As luck would have it, along came his father and Steve in the truck looking for him. He told Steve to back track him and dress out the buck, then drag it up to the truck while he got warm. Fortunately for Steve, the deer was only 100 yards or so away.

When they brought the deer home and had a chance to look him over, the complete story was revealed. This was the buck that Bob had wounded and lost in the morning. Terry had actually missed the buck when his sights were loaded with snow. Seeing blood in the tracks, he had believed he hit him. Finishing him off in the reservoir ended a chase that began at 8 AM, with a lengthy break in between.

The Point System

Terry really enjoys his deer hunting, but he never specifically hunted for a big rack of antlers. Also, he rarely, if ever, carried a camera. About the only thing he ever kept track of was points on his racks that would number consecutively 1 through his highest point rack. So far, he has taken 1 through 10. He's had many 8s, 9s, and 10s, but never higher. Maybe next season!

The Big Gray Rock

Paul Jacobs was Terry's neighbor. He ran The Stillwater Shop for many years. In his early years, Paul hunted and fished in Alaska a lot. In fact, Terry bought a boat from Paul that was used on the Mackenzie River up in the Yukon. Unfortunately for Paul, he was hooked on smoking and he eventually came down with emphysema. Paul could still get around and function, but any strenuous work was very limited.

When Paul was in his 70s, party permits were still available in the Adirondacks. Paul had a permit to fill, but wanted Terry to give him a hand doing it. Terry suggested that he at least go out and try to fill it himself. Paul didn't go out and then it was late in the season with Paul still bugging Terry. The ice was good on the reservoir, with a fair amount of snow cover. Terry agreed to take him out the next day.

In his day, Paul was a good hunter, but frugal in his ways. He would sometimes boast about how long a box of shells would last for him. He was all dressed the next morning, ready for Terry to take him down the reservoir. Terry showed up with his Bombardier Olympic 10.8 hp snowmobile. He towed a small fiberglass toboggan behind to carry their cased rifles. There was nobody around, so they had the whole place to themselves.

Terry decided to try a place down the flow near Devil's Hole, about 4 miles off. Paul got on behind Terry and with rifles and showshoes loaded on the toboggan, off they went. It had snowed and blowed recently. Everything was plastered with snow. The only color in the entire landscape was their yellow snowmobile. At their hunting destination, Terry instructed Paul to snowshoe east for about 10 minutes and then just stay on watch. He watched Paul labor off and then enter the woods. Terry waited 15 minutes more before starting his hunt. He was using a lever-action 30-30 with open sights for this hunt.

When Terry entered the woods, it was truly a "white wilderness." The snow clung to everything. After travelling only 200 yards, he stopped. There was what appeared to be a big gray rock about 100 feet ahead. It seemed so out of place because there was no snow on it. Just to the right of it was a snow laden tree. Through its branches, Terry could see the face of a deer looking at him while chewing. He didn't know if it was buck or doe, and with a permit, who cares? He aimed right for the head and shot. Immediately the head turned and so did this huge set of antlers! When the deer bolted off, the huge gray rock went with it. Wow, Terry couldn't believe it was all one deer. He only tracked it 100 yards when he saw it standing head down and shaking its head. The buck was quartered to him and facing away. Terry shot again, trying to miss the hind quarters and slip one into the rib cage. The buck ran off again. A couple of minutes later, he sees Paul ahead, standing near the tracks. Terry said, "Did you see that deer?" Paul replied, "Yes." Terry said back, "Well, why didn't you shoot it?" Paul then said, "Because he ran out here and hit this sapling and fell down. He was hurting. Then he got up and ran down into that swamp. I wasn't going to waste a bullet on him. He'll be dead any minute now!" Terry thought to himself, "I would have paid you for the bullet, just to be dressing out that buck now!" Terry followed the buck down into the swamp and found it dead under the limbs of a spruce tree. Fortunately, it did not go far.

It was all he could do to drag that buck out and roll it over for dressing. What a monster! It was the biggest bodied deer by far that he had ever taken. The rack was also his biggest. It had a wide spread and carried 10 evenly matched points. Terry was amazed at how heavy it was, especially after the rut. It was brought back to Paul's and hung in his garage. Paul ate off him all winter. Toward spring, he cut off the antlers, cleaned them up, and put them on a plaque. He hung them in the store for everyone to see. About 5 years later, Collin Kellogg spotted the rack in Paul's store. Collin measures racks for the NY State Big Buck Club and Boone & Crockett book. He measured the antlers to satisfy his curiosity. They scored 141 3/8. The dressed buck was never weighed.

What's the Problem?

This story may seem a little unfair to Diane, but these things do happen. I will add that she is also a good shot and has several bucks to her credit. It all began with an evening drive back to Stillwater. Diane was driving along on the hogback when a beautifully racked buck crossed the road in front of her. The sight of that buck made her want to try for him. Once home, she told Terry that she wanted to try for that buck. He replied, "That buck might be miles away by morning, but we can try."

The next day found them out in the same general area where she saw the buck. The snow cover was thin and patchy, so there was no attempt to track. They had tracked many times together with Terry doing the tracking and Diane doing the looking. Today, Terry was following a deer run and looking also. They slowly moved along in an area where there was a lot of small spruce in the understory. On a small rise, he could see a distant hillside. He made 2 short bleats on his call, then saw some movement about 200 yards off on the hill. It was a deer and it began walking their way. He whispered to Diane, "There is a deer coming!"

Diane was carrying a Ruger, lightweight bolt-action in .308 caliber, with a scope on it. Before the season had opened, Terry had reminded her to take the rifle out to check the sights and re-familiarize herself with it. Like many other hunters, she didn't. Meanwhile, the deer was getting closer. Terry whispered back, "It's a buck! An 8- or 9-pointer!" Diane had her rifle up now. The buck, walked through the cover, went below Terry and then arced up, right in front of Diane. He stopped 30 feet from her and then lifted his head, looking at them. Diane had her sights on the buck all the way, and especially at 30 feet. Terry was thinking, "What seems to be the problem here?" Finally the buck wheels and races off with Terry firing one hasty shot that misses.

Terry said, "Why didn't you shoot?" Diane replied, "I don't know! I kept pulling and pulling on the trigger, but it wouldn't go off!" Terry asked, "Is your safety off?" Diane quietly answered, "No."

A Real Noisy Hunt

Terry was telling me that just like in some of my books, hunters would have their best luck in bad weather or hunting conditions. He has had real good luck also when things don't seem so good. He described one hunt that he and Diane went on

Stillwater Reservoir with boat launch, left, and dam, center. The Moshier Reservoir extends to the left below dam. (Bob Elinskas)

Several wooded peninsulas extend into the reservoir from it's south shore. (Bob Elinskas)

where their chances did not appear good at all.

In Late November, Diane and Terry decided to try a hunt off the reservoir. The main body of Stillwater was open, but the bays were beginning to ice over. They headed up the flow in Terry's aluminum boat, while breaking thin ice. You could hear it miles away! What a racket! You swear the boat was going to open up and sink also. With the bad ice, they changed plans. Terry cut the boat in toward shore where they would hunt the Bear Point Peninsula, way short of the Devil's Hole.

Snow conditions on shore were bad. There was a foot of snow cover with a noisy ice crust on top. The crust wouldn't support the weight of a person or a deer. Terry told Diane to walk up to the height of ground where she could watch for deer coming off the peninsula. He would go back to the point and try to push a deer out to her. Terry watched her walk up the ridge toward where she should stand. He then started heading out to the point along the shore. He had covered half the distance when he heard a shot from way off. It seemed too far away to be Diane. Then he reasoned, "There wouldn't be any other damn fools around doing this and Beaver River Station is 5 miles away! It must have been Diane." Instead of going all the way out to the point, he cut in there and went crunching back toward his wife. When 50 yards away, he caught sight of her and she shouts, "Hey, have you got a pen on you that works? Mine is all froze up!" The temperature is down near zero. Diane had a beautiful 8-pointer down. She had only been on watch a little while when the buck came walking right up to her. You can't get a buck sitting home by the fire!

They often hunted together late in the season. On one hunt, over near Stillwater Mountain, Terry shot an 8-pointer in the morning and Diane shot an 8-pointer in the afternoon!

The Doe Bleat Call

When Terry was just a kid (10 or 11 years old), his uncle Andrew was a caretaker for an estate in Rensselaer County. It bordered the Massachusetts state line. His uncle hunted the property and Terry's father was given permission also. They were participating in a drive one day around noon and they had to stay on location at this old pile of logs. His father, Robert, thought it was a good time for a sandwich and a cup from his Thermos. He sat down on a log with Terry and began to dine. Terry then saw him let out 2 bleats with his mouth. He was just a kid and didn't know what to make of it. Then next thing he noticed was Robert looking for a place to put down his coffee cup. Here comes 2 bucks! Bob dropped both bucks on the spot and then stayed put to finish eating lunch. He spoke to Terry, saying, "Mark my words: Someday someone is going to market a deer call that sounds like that!" Ten years later, someone did. The doe bleat call!

Boat launch at Stillwater Reservoir. Terry patrolled this district as NY State Forest Ranger for 31 years, beginning in 1967.

Surprise Buck

Terry uses the deer call occasionally in the woods. He may try it 50 times before he gets any kind of reaction to it. Sometimes he will wonder if it was the call or just by accident that he had some shooting. Deer can hear pretty damn well. This was demonstrated just by accident one day on a hunt with his father. It was late in the day when both Terry and Bob were heading out to their truck. Terry caught a glimpse of his father in the distance through a low spot in a ridge. Rather than shoot, Terry blew on his doe bleat call real loud to get Bob's attention. Shortly afterward, he heard his father shoot twice.

It turned out that Bob didn't hear the call, but a buck in the swamp he was passing by did. He came running out, right into Bob, who quickly took advantage of the situation and dropped the buck. Bob said that he wasn't even hunting. He was tired and heading back to the truck!

Terry and Diane Perkins at their Island home. (Bob Elinskas photo)

A Frank Lamphear Story

I don't think any of my Adirondack books would be complete without at least one Frank Lamphear story. For new readers who have never heard of Frank, he was a big, tough ex-marine and a no-nonsense conservation officer based out of Raquette Lake. He served the state for 32 years in that position, starting in 1950.

During the 1960s, Terry worked for Fish and Wildlife. One November saw him out on patrol in the Moose River Plains with Frank. Frank was checking hunters for proper licenses, tags, and that kind of stuff while Terry was aging deer that had been taken. At this time, Frank was driving a 1958 Ford sedan as his state vehicle. This was the first year the Plains were open to the public.

It was during the course of their rounds that they saw 4 hunters drag an 8-point buck out of the woods and onto the road. All of them were sweating profusely and declaring what a tough drag they endured while removing their trophy from the deep woods. They all guessed the buck's dressed weight at 200 pounds or more. Then they asked the state officials, Terry and Frank, for their professional guess. Frank said, "He's the deer man. There is your expert," pointing at Terry. Terry answered, "I just age them. Unless I have a set of scales handy, I don't get involved with weights!" One hunter said, "Well, he's got to weigh at least 200 pounds!" They turned to Frank, saying, "What do you think he weighs?" Frank said, "I don't think he'll go 200." A hunter said, "Well, by jeepers, you just try to lift him and you may change your mind!" Frank walked over to the buck and grabbed one front leg and one hind leg then picked it up, waist-high. Frank matter-of-factly said, "Yep, about 150." Their jaws dropped about 3 inches when they saw that. It kept a smile on Terry's face the rest of the day.

Trappers Larry Combs and Jim Harter

Larry Combs was raised on a farm in Litchfield Township, Herkimer County. He began trapping when only 8 years old. Larry loved to trap and his passion for the sport has never left him. His adult years saw him trapping the Adirondacks every winter. He belonged to a sporting club up in Hamilton County and he would trap the property in spring for beaver and otter. One evening, Larry stopped at the camp of an acquaintance to play cards. Everyone knew that Larry enjoyed his time spent in the Adirondack back country. The fellow with the camp happened to be a Hamilton County Committeeman. He told Larry, "I've got a great job for you, if you are interested. It's the fire observer's job here in the Long Lake area. The tower is so remote, we can't get anyone to fill the vacancy." Larry replied, "Well, that sounds pretty good to me. Where is it?" Larry began his tour as Fire Tower Observer on Kempshall Mountain in 1967.

Working as an observer in spring through fall left him free to trap all winter. Also, at that time, there was a bounty on bobcats. Larry would catch several cats near his cabin on Kempshall every season. Both Herkimer and Hamilton counties paid a bounty on bobcats. This was a good situation for Larry and he enjoyed his seasonal job on the tower. Sitting up in the tower every day, Larry was keenly aware of any changes going on around him. These may be weather conditions, leaf out progress in spring to fall colors, or smoke from a distant fire.

Larry's view to the northeast included the drainages of Cold River, Pine Brook, and Round Pond. During the late 1960s and into 1970, he could see a dramatic increase in active beaver ponds. This amount of beaver activity would get any trapper excited. Larry wanted to get in there and trap those ponds. He would need a trapping partner to go in with him though. Jim Harter from Mohawk, NY, was a recent addition to the family tree, having married his wife's cousin Sharon that year. Jim was a trapper also, but not on the scale that Larry was. Jim had been trapping muskrats and mink since his school days and really enjoyed it. He had no experience trapping beaver or otter. Larry offered Jim the chance to go in trapping with him as a partner. He would teach him all he needed to know about beaver and otter trapping. Jim enthusiastically agreed, and so the planning began for beaver trapping in February, March, and April of 1971.

In the fall of 1970, both men with their wifes drove up to Long Lake. They had Herb Helms fly them over the Round Pond and Pine Brook area. Each man marked the active beaver colonies on his map. Air charter was cheap in those days.

146   In the Woods with **Adirondack Sportsmen**

The view north east from the top of Mount Kempshall. In late 60s, Larry Combs could see water rising in all the beaver meadows as beaver populations increased. Corner Pond, lower right and Round Pond, center. (Photo by Bob Elinskas)

It cost them $25.00 for their flight. On the return, Jim thought he was going to crap his pants when Herb flew the aircraft right under the Route 30 bridge!

Setting up Camp

Beaver season opened on February 20th in 1971. Before this, the region had experienced a 36 inch snowfall. The trail into the area started 7 miles down the north end of the lake from the bridge. They had to drive their snow machines down empty just to break out a trail to pull their camp and supplies in on. On the day they set up camp, the weather had warmed and it began to rain. It rained hard and steady all the while their plastic tarp shelter was being erected. Both men were soaking wet on completion. They decided not to stay, but to go out and dry off. It had only taken them 30 minutes or so to come in from Long Lake village. Now their trail had turned into a wet, slushy channel. The snowmobiles would sink deep into the wet slush on the return trip. They had hip boots on and were up over their knees in slush and water trying to make progress back toward town. It took them 3 ½ grueling hours to return. Then they found a Laundromat where they took turns staying in the men's room, while the other dried his clothes. They drove home after drying off. Not a fun day!

The camp was just a rough shelter, covered with 2 layers of plastic sheeting. It was a rectangular construction, wide enough on one end for 2 sleeping bags and just high enough to stand up in. The floor was covered with spruce boughs. On the other end, they put their 2 snowmobiles inside and out of the weather. For heat, they had a good-sized white gas stove used for cooking. No wood stove! They used on average 1 gallon of Coleman fuel each week. The burner would produce enough heat to slightly warm the enclosure. A pair of socks would dry if hung high near the ceiling, but their boots would remain frozen near the walls on the floor. They wore felt inserts in the boots and slept with them at night so their feet were always warm. Be it ever so humble, it was home to them and a place to get out of the weather.

Putting Out The Line

The first week saw them building two lines of traps. Larry showed Jim how to make some basic sets for beaver and where to locate them. From then on, it was trial and error. Jim caught on quickly and the traps began to produce. In addition to beaver and otter, they also set traps for fox, coyote, and bobcat. They used beaver carcasses for bait at these. Eventually the 2 lines combined totaled about 100 sets. They had another 36 inch snowfall to contend with and had to break out all their trails again. Traps were set from Round Pond to Cold River and every stream and beaver colony in between.

7 beaver and 1 otter in front of their camp. (J Harter photo)

First beaver caught on Pine Brook. (J Harter photo)

Open water at the outlet of Round Pond. (J Harter photo)

Larry Combs clean skinning a beaver in camp. "After dinner chores." (J Harter photo)

Found By Accident

Jim was walking out into a beaver meadow one day when everything was frozen over pretty tight. Suddenly, he crossed a thin spot and found himself standing in a channel, up to his knees in water. Larry was with him at the time. After looking it over, he told Jim that it would be a good place to put in a set. Larry told him how to build the set and Jim put it in place. They took 3 otter and 2 beaver from this one set!

Jim Harter with an otter caught in the "run" accidently found. (J Harter photo)

The Taj Mahal

Jim was out in a blinding snowstorm one day checking his traps. He was over by Pine Brook on his snowshoes with the snow swirling all about and trying to keep on course to the next set. Suddenly, he heard this loud, gruff voice ring out, "Heeeey!" It sent a chill up his back and made his hair stand up. He wasn't aware of anyone within miles of him. He looked and saw the bewhiskered face of Phil Clark screened through the heavily falling snow. Phil hollers, "This weather isn't fit for man nor beast! You aren't down there on Cold River in that plastic chalet are you?" Jim was a little embarrassed about their shelter then, but he replied, "Yes." Phil replied, "My camp is right over here. How about a hot cup of coffee?" Jim didn't realize he was that close to any camp. When he walked into Phil's tent, he felt like he was walking into the Waldorf Astoria! A warm woodstove, gas lamp, comfortable

2 pole sets and 2 beaver caught. (J Harter photo)

chair and a good cup of coffee! A couple of cozy cots to sleep on, also. No frozen boots in there! He had a great visit with Phil and it was tough to leave, but he had traps to check.

The Sound of Death

One of the things they had to live with in camp was the sound of brush wolves killing deer almost every night. Just about at dark every night, they would hear a pack of them vocalizing their weird howling and yodeling. They would hear them chasing down another deer and then more weird vocalizing. One evening, Larry was coming back toward camp in the dark when the coyotes started in, howling right behind him. It was very unnerving because it sounded like they were very close to him. The lake was nearby, so he ran down onto it and drew his revolver. For a few minutes, it sure sounded like they were after him! He was glad to make it to camp that evening.

Double Trouble

Larry was out checking traps one day when he saw where Phil Clark had made a set for beaver less than 4 feet from one that he had previously made. Both were pole sets, so Larry opened up a hole in the ice to look down and see if his trap

Larry standing next to a beaver lodge. (J Harter photo)

Larry Combs with otter, outlet of Catlin Pond. (J Harter photo)

Larry Combs heading into camp with a blanket beaver. (J Harter photo)

was still there. It was gone and about that time, Phil came walking up to check his trap. Larry opened up the hole to remove the pole and trap, but it didn't want to come out. Both traps were investigated and it was discovered that Larry had caught a beaver by its front foot and when trying to escape, it was caught by a toe on its hind foot in Phil's trap. At least that was their guess. Larry got the beaver! The guys pulled their traps at the end of the season with 70 beaver and over 20 otter to their credit.

The Dark Cloud

Trapping out of a remote camp site was a great adventure for the 2 men. It is something they look back on with pride and enjoyment. The only dark spot on the whole trip were the Fish and Wildlife EnCon officers. They visited 3 times, driving over their snowshoe trails, pulling sets and then leaving them to freeze in.

WILLARD T. RACHA
RAW FURS

Area Code 315
831-3375

REMSEN,
NEW YORK 13438

Bought of **Jim Harter**   Date **April 7/1971**

Address _____

Quantity	Description	Price	Amount
1	super	24 00	24 00
2	blanket	22 00	44 00
5	X large	18 00	90 00
6	large medium	9 00	54 00
4	medium	6 00	24 00
			236 00
4	rats	1.80	7 20
1	otter	35 00	35 00
1	coon	2 50	2 50
			280 70
1	Super	Extra	62 00
5	Blanket	2	342 70
2	XL		171 35
2	L		75 00
1	M		96 35
1	owed for hat		
	$209.	$ 280 70	
		62 00	
2	Blankets	209 00	
1	M	150 00	
3	otter	**TOTAL** 701 70	~~236 00~~
	$150 00		

Receipt for part of their catch.

The only thing they found on the line were 2 number 44 Blake & Lamb long spring traps that "might" possibly be an 1/8 inch over the maximum jaw spread. Really? Like this is some huge advantage over the beaver! It has to be like a state trooper giving everyone a ticket for doing 66 mph in a 65 mph zone. Jim was bringing up legally taken venison from the previous fall all commercially wrapped, but no tag number on it. Citation written! You know if they were eating off a hind quarter hanging out on their tree, or setting too close to a house, or on a dam with a hole torn in it, no problem! But these officials were nit-picking. Law enforcement has an important job to do and we expect them to do it. However, they came in with an attitude of "We are going to write you up on anything, no matter how small." Our conservation officers are appreciated and respected across the state, but this performance did not enhance their image. After court appearances, Larry paid $25 for an illegible trap tag and Jim paid $25 for no license number on venison.

Larry has trapped all over the country and sells his own line of lures and bait. He labels it "Fur Catcher" brand. He sells them nationally and goes to 15 or 16 shows each summer. Many of the shows are out of state so a lot of traveling is involved. Larry told me this business has shut down his trout fishing, because he has to bottle and label lures during trout season. His sales come from all over the United States. Larry lived in Colorado for almost 20 years. He trapped out there as a resident and would come back and trap the Adirondacks. The non-resident license was cheaper to buy here in NY than in CO. He moved back to NY state a number of years ago and now lives in Port Leyden with his wife, Cathy. Yes, he still traps!

Jim lives in Mohawk, NY and runs his own business, Harter Tool and Die. He enjoys deer hunting every season with his son, James. Jim still runs a trapline in the Mohawk Valley area and has expanded into coyote trapping. He takes a lot of pride in seeing his grandson Dylan at age 14 already running some traps for muskrat and mink. Recently, Dylan trapped his first coyote.

Johnny Thorpe

In the fall of 2013, I visited with an 80 year old trapper named Johnny Thorpe. I was guided over to his humble abode at Stony Creek by Ron Robert, a retired EnCon officer who lives in Chestertown. Johnny is a career fur trapper. During Ron's active years, he would occasionally check on Johnny's trapping activities. There were never any serious problems and eventually the two became good friends. Before our meeting, Ron told me that when it came to setting traps and catching fur, there wasn't a better man than Johnny Thorpe in the entire state. At the end of our visit, I was convinced he was right. On my long drive home afterward, my thoughts drifted off to a book I had read in the 1980s. It was written by Donald Jack Anderson and titled, "*Goodbye Mountain Man!*" I thought, "Johnny sure fits that description."

I had a warm, but casual greeting from Johnny. Time had obviously left some marks on the man, but he appeared to be a very young 80. He also didn't carry a lot of extra weight around, indicating he was still physically active. He didn't know what to make of me. However, when he learned that I used to trap, spent quite a lot of time in the wilderness areas, and knew some of his friends, then we visited like 2 kindred spirits. Johnny was "cut from a different cloth," as the saying goes. His heart pumped a percentage of Indian blood, so his bond with nature was extra strong. His grandfather was Sauk and Fox Indian.

John was raised in the Cobleskill area and began trapping muskrats and mink while still in grade school during the war years. Pete Rickard also lived there. Johnny followed him around and spent time at his place whenever he could. Pete was one of the best fox trappers of his time and one of Johnny's personal heros. As young as he was, Thorpe learned quite a lot from "The Old Fox!" There were other trapping legends he would read about in *Fur, Fish, and Game* magazine such as Dailey, O.L. Butcher, Nelson, and Walter Arnold. In later years, he would get to meet and visit with many of these trappers. Johnny didn't want any part of the conventional life. He wanted to trap. His traplines run during high school were producing great money and he knew he could make a good living with it. In 1948, Johnny quit school, left home, and turned professional trapper. He never looked back.

He trapped all season long while living out of wall tents or lumber camps. During the off season, he would work at construction, on farms, dude ranches, or hacking horses just to get by until the trapping season opened again. Johnny was doing OK and loving his life of freedom. He was eventually based out of Stony Creek. There he ran extensive lines for anything that crossed his snowshoe trail that was a legal fur bearer or had a bounty on it.

Johnny had a one room cabin at Knolhurst that he used as a base camp during the early 1950s. He ran a 30 mile snowshoe line in that area that included 5 line shelters. He trapped coyote, bobcat, and fox for their bounty and fur and, of course, beaver, otter, mink and muskrat for fur. There was also a $0.50 bounty on porcupines that the counties would pay in an effort to reduce damage to Hemlock and Beech trees. A tail off the critter was all that was needed to collect. Johnny had already turned in over 300 tails that season. Many of the animals he caught provided bait after being skinned for other target animals. One of his line camps near Cold Pond Flows was actually 2 huge boulders that formed a cave-like enclosure. He was able to build an open fire inside and hang his food stores from a ridge pole hung near the top. The roomy enclosure measured 10' x 20' with a 6' ceiling. It was always a comfortable overnight stay.

Johnny well knew the rules of back country traveling, especially when alone. "Always do the safe way, don't take any foolish chances." In his book, *50 Years a Trapper & Treasure Hunter*," he describes where he paid dearly for a foolish decision:

"On one trip over the line it was getting along towards dark when I came to a tricky creek crossing. The crack of the open water had widened quite a bit since the last trip. Common sense told me to take the time to cut a couple of poles to bridge the gap, but I figured I could jump it one more time.

I had just thrown the pack and carbine across to the other side when the ice gave way! The water was only waist deep and I managed to remain upright. The problem was that the webbing of one snowshoe was hung on a beaver cutting on the bottom. I couldn't pull loose, regardless of how I struggled! I had been stupid not to take the time to cut the poles and pulled an amateur trick of having the shoes strapped to my feet when traveling the ice! When you're alone in the wilderness it's just plain dumb to take chances like this! Pulling off my mitten I grabbed my belt knife, bent over and plunged my upper body down into the water and slashed away at the harness. Cutting myself loose, I crawled out on the ice, grabbed the axe, and headed for the spruce. I had to get a fire going an' damn fast! Ripping birch bark and cutting spruce boughs I managed to get a fire started before my fingers got completely numb. I ran back out on the ice and grabbed the carbine an' pack. Back at the fire, I stripped down in the cold an' wrung the water from my clothing the best I could. I kept throwing on the spruce boughs and wood until I had a hell of a bonfire and spent a half hour jumping up an down an' running around trying to keep from freezing until the clothes got halfway dry.

The Hill Creek camp was a good half mile away, and losing the snowshoe meant I would have to bust trail in near waist deep snow. I would be able to stay up on top a couple of steps then break through a couple more. The one snowshoe was worthless and the heavy pack made the trip next to unbearable. It took me over an hour to make the trip to the camp. My pants an' parka were frozen, however, I was soaked with sweat. I got a fire started, cooked a chunk of beaver meat, and brewed up some tea. This placed me in a better frame of mind, and after putting away a second cup of tea, I set about constructing a showshoe of alder. This consisted of two saplings bent in a half moon that were bound together with my boot laces. The webbing was made by weaving into the frame. A pair of shirt sleeves would serve as a harness. It was a crude affair to say the least, but a "trial run" around the camp convinced me it would serve the purpose – at least until I could make it out to the hard road at Harrisburg Lake the next day."

When Johnny was running road lines with his truck, he would often have up to 300 sets to check. Even though he was young and motivated, it was a grueling task to get them all checked. He would start out at first light and run from one set to another. There was no walking! He wouldn't get back until after dark. Then there was skinning to do late into the evening. After two weeks of this, he would be walking around like a zombie. The fur shed would fill up rapidly, but he earned every stretcher full he put up. Johnny scaled his set numbers way back when he got into his late 40s. He still had a lot of motivation, but not the "bounce back" he used to enjoy.

Johnny Thorpe and Frank King were trapping off the north end of Long Lake in 1971 when Larry Combs and Jim Harter were there. Phil Clark and Frannie Alshimmer were also camped on Pine Brook. The following chapter is taken from Johnny's book, *"50 Years a Trapper and Treasure Hunter"* with his permission.

Frank King and the Cold River Line
By Johnny Thorpe

No essay about Adirondack woodsmen would be complete without mention of my ol' friend Frank King. Frank and I spent a lot of time in the woods for a few years digging ginseng, beaver trapping, and digging for treasure. We even did a little gold dredging together. We spent one season trapping beaver back in Cold River, camping in a log lean-to on Calkins' Creek. That was the year I dropped the snowmobile through the ice on Long Lake. (It's still there on the bottom off Island House.)

Of all the wilderness lines that I have operated on I believe I enjoyed this one the most. Frank and I would run separate lines, meeting back at the camp at night. We would rough skin the beaver and freeze 'em up in a big steel box we kept in back of camp, and then take them out by snowmobile to Long Lake where we stored our trucks.

Phil Clark and Fran Alshimmer, a couple of good beaver trappers, operated south and west of us. They were camped on Pine Creek several miles downstream. Frank and I decided to go visit our new found friends one night, so we fired up the snowmobiles and headed down river. By the time we had pulled into their camp it had started snowing at a pretty good clip. We sat around lying and drinking wine for a while before we decided we'd better be heading back up river. It was dark by now, no moonlight, and the snow was falling hard and fast, completely covering the incoming trail. The lower end of Long Lake is a vast maze of cranberry bogs and without the trail to follow we spent the next three to four hours riding around in circles before we located the river.

The next day turned out to be quite embarrassing. Frank and I had decided to run part of the line together making it easier to break out the trails on the new snow. At one beaver lodge I had a pair of baited conibears set about three feet apart. I had caught a beaver in each one and after removing the first one and resetting, I started on number two. This conibear was fairly new and quite touchy. I was lowering it back through the ice hole when it fired, kicked off the edge of the ice, and caught me around the forearm! This in turn caused me to jump back, stepping down through the hole where I had just reset the first conibear and it nailed me around the ankle. Frank had gone on up the flow to check another colony and I could see him heading back down. I had to work like hell with the setting rope to shuck those traps before he got back. He had a camera with him and I knew damn well if he ever got a photo of me in those traps, he would never have let me live it down!

I guess you could say Frank and his wife Claudia were really country. Frank had built a cabin up on "the mountain" out of Weavertown and never did get around to putting in running water. He would work on road construction during the summer while Claudia took care of the household duties such as repairing trucks, cutting firewood, and hauling water for Frank's shower. Frank had gotten tired of having to go all the way down to the creek to take a bath, so being the clever fellow he was, he took his cuttin' torch and cut an old hot water tank length ways, welded a faucet on, painted it black and bolted it up on the roof of the house. Next he built Claudia a ladder and bought her a brand new bucket so she could haul that water up from the springhole early in the morning for the shower. You sure couldn't say Claudia was lazy. Every time I stopped there she was doing all the little things a woman should do. Things like jackin' up a pickup and changin' a tire, splittin' firewood, makin' up rawhide, or puttin' up a load of logs for the sawmill with the new chainsaw Frank had bought her.

They had an outhouse out back that didn't have a door on it because Frank liked to sit out there in the morning and enjoy looking out over the valley. One Sunday morning he was sitting there minding his own business, reading the *Wall Street Journal*, when a dozen snowmobilers broke out of the woods and came roaring through the backyard. Frank was so upset that he, Claudia, and the kids spent most of a week rerouting the snowmobile trail around the mountain rather than putting a door on the outhouse.

Frank and the family pulled stakes a couple of years later and went to Chicken Alaska, mining gold with Chuck Wyman.

Johnny and Frank had their troubles with the game wardens also. It was almost like they came in specifically for their camp. Jack Carrol and Frank Lamphear were in the group. Jack was making a mighty effort to write up even the smallest item that might be considered a violation. Johnny had replaced the snowmobile that went through the ice with a new one. He had the new registration and sticker with him, but it wouldn't stick well on the cold plastic cowling, so he carried it with him. Citation written. He wrote up about 20 "could be" violations. They had caught 7 deer-killing coyotes and one of the frozen carcasses somehow wound up on the nearby brook. A citation was written for polluting a stream. They wrote up the long spring #44 B & L for 1/8" over the legal jaw spread. The approved standard of measuring legal jaw spread had not been written up as of yet. They liked Frank Lamphear though. He didn't participate in all the theatrics going on. In the end, they paid a fine for not checking a trap within a 24 hour period and some other violation. The rest of the season was very productive. They stretched over 100 beaver and a pile of otter.

Coming of The Fisher
Johnny Thorpe

By the late 50s, the fisher population had reached explosive numbers in Warren and Saratoga Counties. Within two years they had wiped out about every porcupine in the lower Adirondacks. They did the job that the bounty system had not been able to accomplish in twenty years!

Johnny Thorpe and Joe Ferrone by a pile of beaver carcasses trapped in the West Stony Creek country. Many more were left in the woods after being rough skinned. (Thorpe photo)

As luck would have it, I was in on the ground floor so to speak. The fisher were invading much of my old bobcat lines, and I was one of the very few out there trapping during the middle of winter. The first year I lost almost half of my fisher because they were footing themselves in steel traps. After that I went to using #220 conibears on running poles. I still caught a respectable number in cubbies, hanging baits, and springholes, but the running pole was simple and faster. For a couple of years, fisher trapping was almost mind-boggling. I had sets that would take eight, ten, and twelve fisher a season. Sometimes I would take fifteen or twenty in a single trip over the line!

There were only a handful of us taking any amount of fisher in the Adirondacks at the time. Frank Webb operating back in the West Canada lakes, Aggie Becker in Saranac, and Bob Manley and Medor Rabbadu in the northern part of the mountains. The total catch of the state was slightly over five hundred and that was broken down between the five of us!

Fur prices jumped up and of course it didn't take long for all the fair weather boys to become fisher trappers. It got very competitive and indeed downright cut throat! In many cases the cat cubbies that I had built and used for years would have someone else's traps in them. Now,

L to R: Johnny Thorpe, Bob Baker, and Jim Comstock in 1974 with some of their fisher, otter and mink. (Thorpe photo)

I'm by nature kind of an "easy going" ol' boy, unless you stomp on my toes – then I've been known to get upset! Anyway, I ended up smashing up a lot of traps and cubbies before I got the message across. I never did mind competition, in fact I thrive on it, but at least a man could build his own sets!

All Over The Country, Canada Too!

Johnny had a number of trapping partners down through the years. All of them good trappers. He trapped Vermont, Maryland, and Virginia. In Virginia, he hooked up with Jim Comstock of Glens Falls. They got into some contract trapping for some large pulp companies. They were taking several hundred beavers a season. Then the Fish and Game Dept. tied them into a company that owned water-rights on Lake Anna. This company provided them with a boat and operator along with 2 men to carry beaver and hand them sticks. The lake had 300 miles of shoreline and they could take beaver in any manor they wished. In 2 weeks they had taken 443 beaver! They ended up selling over 600 beaver and several hundred coon.

He trapped Canada for 2 seasons. One year was a bust, ending when his home burned down in Luzerne. The other year was very successful in taking mink,

Johnny Thorpe with some of his southwest fox, bobcat and coyote pelts. (Thorpe photo)

fox, beaver and otter. On this trip, he took one clever red fox that made him pay dearly for it. Johnny had 6 grouse hanging from the ridge pole inside his line tent. During his absence, a very bold red fox came in and dined on the grouse. That was a clever insult to a professional like Johnny, so on leaving camp, he left the tent door canvas loose with a bedded trap just inside. On return he got the fox alright, but the fox had ripped the whole front of the tent off while tethered on the trap!

The coming years would see him trapping in Colorado with its heavy snow areas and no-snow regions. Then it was off to one of the strangest areas he ever attempted to trap, the desert southwest. While down there, he saw a bumper sticker describing the area, "30 Miles From Water, 2 Foot From Hell." He thought, "How true that is!" Nothing but sand, cactus, and rocks. No water or trees anywhere. He learned how to successful trap this country, though. Learning what worked and

Johnny Thorpe, professional trapper. (Photo compliments of JT)

what wouldn't and where to put his steel. He paid his dues! In Arizona, New Mexico, and even California. Johnny racked up some real impressive catches of bobcats, coyotes, and fox in all 3 states. He returned to NY State in the mid-90s and lives in Stony Creek. At 80 years of age, he can still squeeze a trap spring and runs a modest line! In today's high-tech generation and current regulations, it is very doubtful we will ever see another Johnny Thorpe. He could very well be NY State's last "Mountain Man." Johnny ended his book "*50 Years a Trapper*" with this "Ode to a Coyote":

Ode to a Coyote
By Johnny Thorpe

Born to be a sheep killer,
An' a general all round pest;
But I hate to kill you partner,
Cause you are part of our old West.
You an' me is sorta' actors.
With our backs again' the wall,
In a play that's nearly over–
An' the curtain about to fall.

**Good Bye,
Good Luck,**
I'm gone…

Mule Train

First let's talk about mules. The basic mule is a hybrid cross between a male donkey and a female horse (mare). There are many other ways to breed mules; this is just the "CliffsNote" version! The mule inherits it's incredible strength, intelligence and surefootedness from the donkey, and its beauty and athletic ability from the horse. They can also be bred for size or suitability for the job you want them for. Mules are commonly used for driving, packing, and hiking companions.

Alan Morgan is a houndsman. He lives in the farm country south of Cazenovia where he also keeps some livestock. The livestock includes a pair of mules that he added in 1992. The mules are very versatile. You can use them for occasional work around the farm or draw out logs with them. He has one that goes coon hunting with him, too. I found that a little hard to believe at first. Alan said, "You can ride them right to the tree the hounds are barking up. If you come to a barbed wire fence they will jump right over it. When the shooting is over, they carry out the coons." Not all mules are this cooperative though. They all have their own temperament. You have to find the ones that will do what you want.

Alan hunts with a group of friends primarily from the Remsen area. Nicest bunch of guys you would ever want to meet. They do most of their hunting locally, in and around Remsen. This small community is known statewide for its annual Remsen Barn Festival of the Arts, held in late September amid the fall colors. Just recently, Remsen resident Erin Hamlin brought the town some international fame when she became the first American ever to win a medal in singles luge at the Winter Olympics in Sochi, Russia.

The idea for an Adirondack deer hunt came up while a number of the group were doing volunteer work on the Remsen railroad station. John Secor, Rodney Morgan and Kirk McLaughlin were working there. Taking a week off after the project ended to go deer hunting was in some ways considered a reward for their contributions.

Where to go?

During the 1990s, the state was actively buying large parcels of private holdings to add to the Forest Preserve, in addition to conservation easements. Years earlier, Rodney Morgan (Alan's cousin) had worked on a hunting camp on leased land north of Long Lake. He remembered seeing some real nice bucks taken off the property. Now this tract of land had recently been sold to the state and was open to the public to hunt. He suggested they set up a tent and hunt there. It sounded like their best bet, so plans were made for a hunt in the fall of 1998.

Not What Rodney Remembered

John, Rodney, and Kirk drove up to the area for a week's hunt. The entire area looked different to Rodney now. Before the property was signed over to the state, it was virtually clear cut. The country had grown up to whips and brush. In addition, the logging roads he used to drive in on were now all barricaded. They brought their camping outfit in on a 2-wheeled hand cart. The biggest obstacle to hunting the area was all the thick new growth. Even if you saw a deer in it, you would have to shoot through whips to hit it. At the end of a week, they had taken one big bodied 6-point buck. Their trip was enjoyable though, if not very productive. Camping with good friends and exploring a new area was all worth the effort. They filled the rest of their deer tags in the Remsen area as usual. However, when the remainder of their group heard about the camping trip, they also wanted to try it. Plans were made for a second trip that would include most of their group.

Hee Haaaw!

The area that John, Rodney and Kirk had camped at was 6 miles in from the gate. Bringing in a camp with provisions for 6 or 7 men would amount to a sizable project. Alan had heard that a fella up in the Star Lake area was packing in supplies with mules. APA regulations stated you can't take a horse off a designated horse trail in the park, but a mule isn't a horse. It would be great if Alan's mules could haul their outfit in and out. They called up the district ranger and then he called Albany. Albany replied, "Mules are a kind of 'gray area,' so let them through the gate." In reality the mules and wagon did no damage whatsoever. It also brought the guys into an area that saw little use by others. Even though the deer hunting was much better around Remsen, the week to 10-day Adirondack hunt became a tradition. Alan's rig for hauling in supplies consisted of a fore cart with a trailer hitch welded to it. A standard 4-wheeled wagon was then hitched to the fore cart and, of course the mules or a mule, harnessed to the fore cart. The first trip in with the whole group, Alan used a single mule to pull in the wagon. After that, he used a team. A comfortable camp was hauled in and set up with a minimum of effort. After the hunt, everything was hauled out, plus any deer. There was nothing left to mark their presence. Five men had participated in the hunt during the second year, which was also the first year using a mule. They brought out 4 bucks at the end of their stay.

Robert J. Elinskas 169

The fore cart and Daisy, the wagon gets hitched behind. L to R: Alan Morgan, Rodney Morgan & Herb Morgan. (Secor photo)

Base camp all set up and ready for the hunt. (Secor photo)

Venison to go, ready for the trip out. (Secor photo)

That first year in with the mule was their best season to date. Although fewer deer were taken on later hunts, the Adirondack environment always added its own unique flavor to each trip. Alan spotted a deer in the thick whips one day. It was only 30 feet off the skid trail and appeared to be a spike horn. He shot the buck right in the white throat patch and dropped it cleanly. When he walked into the whips to pull out his buck, the spike turned out to be a 10-pointer! He couldn't make out the rack through all the whips.

The clear cutting plus a series of summer microburst storms that hit made their area incredibly difficult to hunt in any traditional way. One day they tried to push a 50- acre parcel of whips and windfalls. It was so thick no one came out even close to where they were supposed to. Most of their hunting was done along skid trails and beaver meadows. It took time to learn where they all went and what ones would bring you back toward camp. Radios were used to keep in touch and usually only after someone shot.

Bull Frog Buck

Alan found a huge scrape one day that seemed like it was getting a lot of attention. He didn't tell anyone about it and made up his mind to spend a lot of time watching it. Another one of the party had a tree stand across the logging road and up on a little ridge not very far from his watch. It was one of the few trees big

Off to a great start! 11/10/02 Alan Morgan's Bull Frog 10-point buck, taken near dark with a "Texas Heart Shot." (Secor photo)

enough in the entire area that you could hang a stand on! Alan watched the area of the scrape until the light was almost gone. Then he heard the sound of a bull frog croaking off in the whips. He thought, "What is a bull frog doing out this time of the year?" The "frog" moved all the way around him and then stepped out in the skid road. By then, Alan knew it was a buck and now he could make out its rack, but nothing else. It was really too dark to shoot, but he had this buck in front of him. Then he could hear the tree stand hunter coming down from his platform. The buck heard him, too, and raised his tail. Alan could see that alright. Boom! The buck dropped right in the skid trail. The shot also scared the crap out of the tree stander. He thought he was being shot at!

John Secor has had most of his luck deer hunting by going out into a promising area, then sitting down and using his grunt call. There was one area not far from camp that looked good to him. He didn't have long to wait one morning, when a buck and a doe started moving his way aggressively. John shot at the buck through the whips and wounded it in the front leg. This buck ran over past Tim Dunn, but he wasn't sure if it was the deer John had just shot at (couldn't see the head). John got the guys together to see if they could collectively finish it off. First

John Secor at camp with his 8-pointer, 165 lbs. Took 7 guys 5 hours to get wounded buck. (Secor photo)

they waited 2 hours to see if the buck would stiffen up or die. Alan did the tracking and soon found out the buck was still very active. The rest of the guys (6 of them) tried to cut off the wounded buck. At one point, he passed within 50 yards of the tent! The buck was spotted on several occasions, but safety concerns prevented them from taking a shot. With 7 hunters after one buck, you don't want to make a tragic mistake. Alan finally had a clear shot at the buck and safely put him down. All agreed that getting this buck was a community effort!

John grunted one buck into him years back that was the biggest racked buck (dead or alive) that he has ever seen. He only had a head shot, so he tried to keep his cool and carefully squeezed off one shot. He missed it and a sight check later showed his rifle shooting a foot low at that range. Damn!

Missed Opportunities

Rodney's father, Herb, was a heavy smoker and had emphysema. Rodney offered to take him hunting in the Adirondacks. Herb replied, "And how am I supposed to get back in there?" You know I can't do much anymore!" Herb rode in behind Alan's mules. There was a big scrape not far from the tent site. Herb decided

Alan and Rodney Morgan with mules. (Secor photo)

Mule Train bringing in the camp. (Secor photo)

he would spend his days watching that scrape. Since he wasn't far from the tent, he decided to have his lunch there. One day after returning from lunch, he saw where a buck had freshened up the scrape while he was lunching at the tent!

On another day, they dropped off Herb near a big bank of dirt. He was told to sit and watch this area. There were always fresh tracks showing up there. On the way back, Herb was gone, but there was a fresh bear track walking right up to where he had been sitting. He had walked back to camp a little too early!

Buried

In 2003, the mules hauled their camp in over bare ground. The camp was set up and the traditional Adirondack hunt began. There was no tracking snow to date, but there was tracking snow in the forecast for Wednesday evening. The predictions they heard were 6-8 inches. It began snowing around mid-morning on Wednesday and intensified after dark. The men were warm and dry in camp, looking forward to a good night's sleep, but they didn't get it. The wind increased and blew strong all night, rattling the tent fly and walls until first light. They weren't aware that two low pressure areas had combined and was dumping heavy snow over their area. When they awoke Thursday morning, 28 inches of snow covered the ground. John Secor had waded into the snow for an accurate measurement.

Tent will sleep 6 people comfortably. Lee Green, front and Rodney Morgan, rear. (Secor photo)

Difficult walking in 28 inches of snow! (Secor photo)

Opening up a road through the deep snow with the fore cart. (Secor photo)

Breaking trail with the fore cart — looking back the wheel tracks are still 10 inches above the road bed. (Secor photo)

After breaking 6 miles of road open with the fore cart, the camp is loaded and ready to go. (Secor photo)

Now what do we do? It is pretty tough to hunt in crotch deep snow. They didn't know if even more snow was coming. It was decided they would "call it quits" and try to get the camp out. They were 6 miles in from their trucks. Even their team of mules couldn't pull a loaded wagon through all that snow. Alan decided to take the mules with the fore cart and break a trail out to the trucks. He would do that and then take the camp out the next day. Alan's mules were in good physical condition because he had been logging with them prior to this hunt. However, after busting out a trail through all that snow with just the fore cart, they were exhausted! The next day brought warmer temperatures and the snow settled a few inches. The camp was taken down and loaded on the wagon. They didn't push the mules on the way out. Before reaching the trucks they met Ben's wife, Katey, cross-country skiing in. She was hoping to catch them before the camp was down. She told them that a big warm up was coming and all the snow would be gone in the next couple of days. It was too late, though. 2003 was a bust in the Adirondacks!

Team Work

In 2005, most of their hunting group had left for home. Alan, Rodney Morgan, and Ben Secor remained to hunt a few more days. They had good weather with a 2 inch snow cover. They decided to hunt as a team with one man pushing a block of cover and 2 men posted on watch. Alan pushed out 2 pieces then Ben pushed out a couple. All for naught. When Rodney began his push, things began to happen. He ran into a whole bunch of fresh deer sign. He alerted the watchers by radio and then tried to figure out just where the deer were. As he moved through the piece, he could see some movement of deer. They should be breaking out to Ben shortly. Then this doe came racing back through the short spruce trees. He caught a glimpse of a real nice buck behind the doe, but not long enough to get a shot off. Behind him, only a few yards back, was a skid trail, so Rodney quickly moved back where he could look down the length of it. The doe appeared quickly going down the road and then into the whips. Then the buck appeared on the run. Rodney was ready and shot quickly. The buck fell dead in the road, much to Rodney's relief. It was a grand old buck with 10 even points and dressed out 178 pounds. That buck almost came out to Ben, but it turned and followed the doe. It later scored 139 5/8.

The Trouble with Mules

Some years they would haul in the camp and set it up a week before the actual hunt. This was the case one season when they were all into camp by late morning and heading off to hunt by noon. It was cold weather with 2 inches of snow cover. By day's end, everyone was back to camp, but the mules were gone. Alan wasn't overly concerned about it, figuring they were just down the road by the bridge. After supper, Alan and cousin Rodney started tracking the mules back down the road. The mules walked all 6 miles out to the trucks and then an additional 3 miles over to some buildings. Now the temperature had fallen 10 to 20° below zero! After a long day of driving up, hunting all afternoon, and a 9 mile walk after mules, now it was 9 miles back to camp. Alan walked ahead of the mules and Rodney walked behind them. On the way back, Rodney's Mountain Dew, which was under his shirt jacket, froze solid. Then Alan noticed him wandering all over behind the mules. He was falling asleep on his feet! Are we having fun yet? They stumbled into camp at 3 AM. Rodney's beard was frosted snow white and Alan's leg muscles were jumping with spasms.

The Run Away

Two days later, Alan and Rodney met up in the woods. While they were visiting, they saw a crotch horn buck come running by. They both began shooting at it. It went down, got up and ran some more before they finally killed it. Alan went back to camp and brought the mules in with the fore cart. The buck was taken to camp on the fore cart. At camp, the buck was put on the back of the wagon and

Rodney Morgan, 178 lbs, neck shot with 270. 11/19/05 (Secor photo)

then the fore cart hooked up to the wagon. Out on the road, in front of camp, someone decided it was a great place to take a picture of deer, wagon, mules, and hunters. One of their group had a rifle with a hair trigger on it. It was so sensitive it was known to go off while just loading a round into the chamber. Everyone was uncomfortable around it. This rifle was laid across the wagon while everyone got into position for the photo op. Mules can sometimes be "flighty." They get this from the horse side of their genes. It was during the photo op that their flighty horse genes surfaced. As soon as the first photo was taken, the mules bolted off down the road as fast as they could run. Alan and the buck fell off, Rodney was hanging on by his fingernails, and John Pinkos ran and grabbed the reins. The reins were wrapped around the uprights on the fore cart, so pulling on them wouldn't do any good. He was pulled along faster than he could run, looking like Superman flying to the rescue! He bounced 3 times on the road after letting go! Rodney slowly worked his way forward, not unlike heroes in the Wild West movies that stopped the run-away stagecoach horses. He jumped from wagon to fore cart, grabbed the reins forward of the uprights and brought the mules under control. Fortunately, the safety on the "hair trigger" rifle held after bouncing around on the trailer bed during the wild ride. Nobody had a clue or a guess as to what started the mules. Sweet Pea and Daisy were perfectly normal after that.

Photo taken of Rodney and his 4-point just before the mules ran off with everything. Rodney was able to Wild West style, work his way up front and stop the mules. L to R: Ben, Alan, Rodney & John Pinkos, mules Daisy & Sweet Pea. (Secor photo)

The first of 2 loads Alan Morgan driving Daisy & Sweet Pea, had a roll over a little while later. (Secor photo)

Those Damn Beavers

On one trip into camp with the mule team, their wagon, loaded with tent, gear, and food, rolled over. Beaver had dammed up a stream that ran near the access road; the dam construction ran part way onto the road. Alan thought if he just rolled the wagon slowly over it, all would be OK. It wasn't! At the height of the dam, the wagon rolled over onto its side, like in slow motion. Everything had to be set aside, the wagon rolled upright, and then repacked. The only thing broken was 2 eggs! Alan acknowledged that the load might have been a little top-heavy. There were 2 loads going in that day and this was the biggest. Their camp is very comfortable and they eat real well!

No Coyotes Allowed

Alan had a mule into camp named "Dick." This mule would not tolerate coyotes. At home, if any coyotes came into his pasture, Dick would run them right off. The same held true for deer camp. If any coyotes came around during the night, Dick would get right after them. Alan would sometimes see Dick's tracks up to 2

Fall of 2001, the trailer rolled over in slow motion due to a slant in road. Only thing broken were 2 eggs. (Secor photo)

miles from camp chasing coyotes. He would always be back by morning though.

2005 was the last year they used mules. The bridges they crossed on the way in were becoming unsafe and Alan didn't want to risk his mules. Their tradition continued with the use of 2-wheeled deer carts and lighter tents and equipment.

The Sociable Mrs. Moose

Rodney and Ben were the only ones at camp one day and decided to work together for a buck. During that hunt, Ben describes how he met Mrs. Moose.

"We decided to do some little pushes to each other, so I stayed put for a while and sent Rodney around to get on watch. Just about the time Rodney got around to where he was going to watch, I had a deer blow at me and caught a glimpse of one or two going kind of in the wrong direction. I decided to follow their tracks if I could, so I radioed Rodney and had him move to a different watch. I started down in the swamp where the deer headed, and pretty soon, I had all kinds of deer tracks, but none that were too impressive. I started following some in the direction of Rodney and then all of the sudden I had fresh moose tracks in the snow. The moose was heading the same way as the deer and the moose tracks were much easier to see in the little bit of snow and moss in there. I hadn't gone very far and I found

"Dick" mule, No Coyotes allowed! (Secor photo)

a fresh pile of moose scat, then another and another. I knew that the moose had definitely spent some time in there and was most likely living right there in that swamp. I followed the tracks a little further and found a fresh moose bed, no snow in it, but I hadn't heard the moose go out, and it was just a walking track going out of there and more piles of scat. I hadn't gone far from the bed and all of a sudden, I could hear something coming toward me. I got my gun up to where I figured the animal was going to step out, and pretty soon I had this big cow moose filling up my scope at about 30 yards and closing. I put my rifle down a little disappointed that it wasn't some big ol' nasty swamp buck, but at the same time pretty tickled to see a moose in the ADKs. She kept walking toward me, so when she got to about 20 yards, I started moving around a little bit and talking to her, so she would know I was there. Well, she saw me, but didn't quite know what I was and kept coming closer. When she got to 10 yards, she finally stopped, but didn't seem too bothered by my presence. I kept talking to her and told her what I was up to while I got my

Going in for a full week. 11/7/09 (Secor photo)

day pack off and dug around for my camera. After I took a few pictures of her, I got on the radio and told Rodney I was 10 yards from a moose, just standing there. He asked where I was and said he'd like to see her too, so he started my way. Mrs. Moose and I waited patiently for about 10 minutes or so, and then we heard Rodney coming through the swamp. I guided him in and he got to about 30 yards from us and she still stood there. After we had seen enough and the moose walked away from us a little bit, we decided to leave her be and check out a different area for deer.

As it turned out, Rodney's son Rick had been in that same general area 2 weeks earlier and had been grunting when she came to him. He had his camera phone with him, but the SD card was full, but the moose waited while Rick deleted some old pictures off his phone and took a few of her. Rodney knew about Rick's encounter, but didn't realize I hadn't heard about it. Rick had also had a trail camera in that area for a couple of months and had a picture of a cow and a calf moose. We never saw any signs of the calf, so who knows what happened to it."

The Beginning of a Streak

No one enjoyed the Adirondack hunts more than Ben Secor. He was the youngest of the group and also one of the unluckiest. He has taken plenty of bucks in the Remsen area, but the Adirondack bucks kept eluding him. In 2007, due to a

A sociable cow moose walks up to Ben Secor. (Secor photo)

Mrs. Moose (Ben Secor photo)

The new lightweight camp after the mules were discontinued in 2006. (Secor photo)

hunting trip to Colorado, he had missed the main traditional hunt after Election Day. Now after Thanksgiving weekend, Ben and Lee Green hiked in to hunt for a weekend. The two men brought their camp and gear in on a Friday afternoon with a 2-wheeled deer cart. About 5 miles in, they came to a long straight section of the road. Ben spotted what appeared to be a deer in the road about 250 yards off. He removed his rifle from its case and looked through the scope. It was in fact a deer and a buck also. Lee also had his scope on it and confirmed it to be a real good buck. Ben had loaded his rifle so he rested it across the deer cart and fired. The buck ran off the road.

    They moved on down to where the deer had been and Ben saw the buck go out in the nearby whips and fired again. There was hair in the road on the tracks, but no blood until he started tracking. Then there were just a few drops. Ben started tracking the buck and Lee tried to cover areas where it might cross a road. Ben could hear the buck going out ahead of him, but never got to see it. At 3 PM, the temperature was down near zero and camp was still on the deer cart. They quit the track until the next morning.

    He jumped this buck again in the morning only 100 yards from where he quit the track on Friday. There was about 4 inches of snow with a light crust on top, so he could hear the deer and it could hear him. The buck led him in circles, around swamps and, at one point, into some fairly open hardwood whips where he could see almost 100 yards. The buck always stayed just out of sight. Ben remembered reading one article that said, "If they run, you run." He tried that and it did not work! He stopped briefly to have a sandwich. Afterward, he saw where the buck had bedded only 50 yards away during his lunch. The beds did seem to be getting closer together, so Ben kept pushing him. Eventually, the buck headed for a lake where the shoreline brush was short.

The tracks led out through this brush to the frozen lake, but no deer could be seen. At the lake edge, Ben found broken ice and about 15 feet out, the buck's head stuck out of the water. No signs of life. He put his day pack and rifle down then went looking for a stick to hook his antlers with and pull him to shore. As soon as he started toward him with the stick, the buck jumped up and started breaking ice out into deeper water. This was a real shock to Ben, who went running back for his rifle and put another bullet into him. The buck did a little side stroke circle and actually came in closer to shore before he died for real. Ben was able to hook an antler and haul him in. It took about 24 hours and 7 or 8 miles of tracking to actually tag this buck. This was his first Adirondack buck, an 8-pointer. He had finally broken a 7 year drought! Ben has filled his tag on Adirondack bucks for 5 years straight now.

Crossing Points

The boys had made many trips over the 6 mile stretch of road to their camping spot. Always noticing any deer activity along or crossing their route. Earlier in the 2009 season, Ben and Kirk McLaughlin had spotted a big track crossing the road and a good-sized tree all freshly rubbed up. Later in the season, Ben was coming in with his father, John. It was snowing hard as they pushed the loaded deer cart in. When they got to the area where Ben and Kirk had seen the big track and rub, there were deer tracks crossing again. These were mostly filled in with the heavy snow, but Ben thought they had to be less than an hour old. He left John out by the road and took the track. Ben kept John informed of his whereabouts with the radios, so he could move up or down the road as needed. Ben tracked the buck through some real thick stuff, with snow hanging all over the spruce and whips. He was thinking that he was never going to see that buck down in this stuff. Then he stepped into a deep hole, pulled himself out, and walked around a short spruce tree. There was the buck standing and looking at him, only a short distance off. He could only see one antler, but it was a big one. Ben quickly shot just as the buck was turning to run. He dropped right there and it was over. When he walked over to the buck, there was one perfect antler in the air with 5 points. The other was buried in the snow. Before he pulled the other half out, he pessimistically thought, "I'll probably get a deformed other half or only 2 or 3 points on it!" But it was a perfect match. He got John on the radio and told him he shot a 10-pointer. John answered, "Did you stab it? I didn't hear any shots!" With all the snow, the shot was very muffled.

End of the Day Buck

Camp is usually set up shortly after Election Day in November. This is also when Adirondack bucks are on the move. They set the "big top" up one fall when the weather had warmed into the 50s. The little snow cover that remained was rapidly disappearing. By 3 PM, camp was all set up and ready for the busy week ahead. Ben Secor left camp to check out a few places before dark. Near dark, he was in an area where he had tracked a nice buck the year before. There was a small vly with an old beaver dam on it. There was also a real nice buck track crossing here. Ben started thinking, "It might be a good place to watch, especially late in the day."

The next morning he returned and built himself a small blind to watch from. He left afterwards to check out a few more spots he was interested in. Late in the afternoon, he returned to watch from his blind. His view was limited to barely 100 feet due to all the thick cover. Around 4:15 PM with low light levels becoming prevalent, Ben noticed 2 or 3 Canada Jays fly out from the brush near the old beaver dam. There was a deer trail that ran down towards the dam also, and he thought he

Ben with his perfect 10-pointer. L to R, back: Kirk McLaughlin & John Secor; front: Lee Green, Rodney Morgan, Ben Secor & John Pinkos. (Secor photo)

could hear something move occasionally. Finally, he saw some movement, and at first it looked like someone wearing a yellow vest. Then the deer turned and he could make out a fine set of antlers. It was tough to see the buck's body through the whips and gathering darkness. In an effort to get him into his shooting lane, Ben grunted twice with no reaction and then he used his doe bleat can. No reaction either. Finally, he stood up and he could see the buck's eye looking his way. It was the only part of the deer (except the rack), he could see in the poor light. Ben aimed for the eye, since it seemed to be a now or never, and shot. Nothing moved! The deer was still there. He shot again, with the same results. Ben moved a short distance off to his right where he could see better and incredibly, the buck was still there standing broadside! He shot again quickly, wounding the buck. The deer ran off into the whips, leaving a blood trail. It was almost dark now, so Ben returned to camp for help and lights.

He was back on the track about 2 hours later with Rodney Morgan, Rick Morgan, Lee Green, and John Pinkos. The buck would intermittently bleed, but they were able to follow the track. It led them down near an active beaver pond where they heard beaver slapping the water with their tails. Ben had visions of the buck walking out into the pond, but he didn't. They would occasionally hear the

L to R: Rodney Morgan, Rick Morgan, John Pinkos & Ben Secor with his buck. 11/8/09 185 lb 10-point (Secor photo)

buck go out ahead of them on leaving its bed. He was hurt bad, but it was still quite possible they could lose him. They had been tracking this buck for 1 ½ hours, and now the beds were getting closer and closer. Ben was in the lead doing the actual tracking, but he wasn't the only one on this blood trail! Behind their group was a very vocal pack of coyotes. As the hunters moved along the trail, so did the coyotes. They kept about the same respectable distance behind throughout the tracking job. Ben's buck finally ran out of blood and they recovered him. He was a big 10-point that dressed out at 185 pounds. They didn't dare leave him in the woods because of the coyotes, so he was brought out after dressing. The coyotes had the gut pile all cleaned up by morning!

The traditional Adirondack hunt continues after 17 years and counting! What will next season bring?

Other books by the author:

A Deer Hunter's History Book
Adirondack Camps & Hunts
A Taste of Wild Alaska
Hunting Central New York White Tails
Adirondack Hunters and Trappers

They can be found at Barnes & Nobles Booksellers, many outlets throughtout the Adirondacks, and North Country Books in Utica, NY.